FIFTY YEARS AGAINST THE STREAM

Owing to the antiquity and rarity of this book, certain pages are regrettably absent, and readability is compromised due to the blurring of the original text. If you possess any insights regarding the availability of these missing sections, kindly inform us. Your assistance is crucial in ensuring the completion of this significant work for the benefit of future generations.

FIFTY YEARS AGAINST THE STREAM

THE STORY OF A SCHOOL IN KASHMIR 1880 - 1930

E. D. TYNDALE-BISCOE

GYAN

Published by

Gyan Publishing House
5, Ansari Road
Daryaganj, New Delhi-110002
Phone: 011-47034999, 9811692060
E-mail: books@gyanbooks.com

Distribution Network
gyanbooks.com
India, USA, Canada, UK, Australia

ISBN: 978-93-7447-409-9 (PB)

First Published, 1930

2nd Impression 2026

Printed at: Gyan Press, Delhi.

FIFTY YEARS AGAINST THE STREAM:
THE STORY OF A SCHOOL IN KASHMIR 1880 - 1930
Author: E. D. TYNDALE-BISCOE

FIFTY YEARS AGAINST THE STREAM

FIFTY YEARS AGAINST THE STREAM

The Story of a School in Kashmir

1880—1930

BY

E. D. TYNDALE-BISCOE

FOREWORD BY

LORD BADEN POWELL, G.C.M.G., G.C.V.O., LL.D., F.R.G.S.

MYSORE:

PRINTED AT THE WESLEYAN MISSION PRESS

1930

THE SCHOOL MOTTO AND CREST

WE mean by a man, one who is at once strong and gentle, self-reliant and self-sacrificing. The Crest embodies and the Motto proclaims this, our School's ideal of manhood. The paddle stands for self-reliance and sturdy hard work, while its broad heart-shaped blade for large-hearted sympathy and fellow-feeling. The paddles are laid across to remind all men of Him who made self-sacrifice the bedrock of His life and purpose, and service to mankind the one dominating motive of His earthly existence.

—A. S. WADIA.

FOREWORD

'A SMILE and a Stick will carry you through most difficulties in this life.'

If you don't believe that slogan try it yourself, and you will find its truth—with the reservation that, in nine cases out of ten, the smile alone will do the trick.

If you need a concrete example of this truth you will find it in the following story of Fifty Years Against the Stream. The wonderful success achieved by that great work of developing the bodies, the character and the souls of an otherwise feeble people, should give an inspiring encouragement to others faced with apparently unsurmountable obstacles.

The smile, that is the cheery sense of humour, backed by the 'stick' of forceful determination, is the key to Tyndale-Biscoe's success in what he himself describes elsewhere as 'putting backbone into jellyfish'—an adventure in which he deserves the support of all who admire manly, self-sacrificing service, in a far-away outpost of our Empire.

Baden-Powell

PREFACE

TO those who have co-operated with me in producing this short history, I wish to express my deepest thanks.

To the Rev. S. E. Hickox and Miss H. L'E. Burges, for giving many hours of careful work in correcting errors in style, and for their valuable criticism.

To Commander C. E. Eldred, R.N., for the delightful design which graces the cover.

To Pandit Narain Das, for his reminiscences of the early days; and to my father, for supplying me with numerous anecdotes and details.

To my wife, for taking on the tedious job of correcting the proofs.

To Pandit Govind Koul, for the hours he spent in typing the manuscript.

Lastly, to Pandit Shenker Koul, the headmaster, and his Staff, whose years of hard work, suffering and bravery in the face of persecution, have produced something worth writing about.

E. D. TYNDALE-BISCOE.

CONTENTS

LIST OF ILLUSTRATIONS

OF THE STREAM UP WHICH WE TRAVEL

MANY people have heard of Kashmir, and are acquainted with its far-famed beauty through the numerous books that have been written about it; still, perhaps a few words of explanation may be useful before plunging into the main narrative of this book.

First it would be as well to focus the mind's eye on to the extreme north of India, up among the towering Himalayas; there, where the three empires of Russia, China and India meet, is the feudatory State of Jammu and Kashmir. Lying in among these mountains, 5,000 ft. above the sea, is a flat-bottomed valley, about one hundred miles long by forty broad. This is the far-famed Vale of Kashmir. A broad river, the river Jhelum, meanders slowly through the length of the valley, connecting up with numerous placid lakes; while all round the plain rises a ring of towering snow-capped peaks. Kashmir is an extraordinary mixture of the Norfolk Broads and Switzerland.

The journey up to Kashmir from India is a most marvellous contrast; for besides the scenery, the dresses, houses, and boats are quite unlike anything one sees on the two-day train journey over the plains of India, from Bombay to Rawal Pindi in the Punjab. Rawal Pindi is the nearest railway station to Kashmir, and it is there necessary to hire a car and drive the two hundred miles into Kashmir. The road winds through the most wonderful mountainous country; it climbs to 6,000 feet, then it drops down to about 2,000 feet to join the gorge of the Jhelum river. Thence it twists and turns along sheer hillsides, with the Jhelum foaming and roaring hundreds of feet below. Ever upward goes the road, till at last the gorge widens out into the broad smiling valley of Kashmir proper. The Jhelum, now no longer a furious cauldron, becomes a placid river, the patient beast of burden for countless boats.

For thirty miles or so the road runs straight, along magnificent avenues of poplars, passing picturesque Kashmiri villages, the thatched and sloping roofs of their houses peeping out among the clumps of walnut and chenar trees. At last, the long drive over, one reaches the capital city of Srinagar, which is just about fifty miles up stream from Baramulah, the town situated at the point where the Jhelum changes from peace to fury.

Srinagar is practically in the centre of the valley, and its position can be located from many miles away by the Takht-i-Suleiman hill, which rises up 1,000 feet out of the plain close to the city. On the top of the Takht is an ancient Hindu temple, which is illuminated at night with flood-lights, so that even in darkness it is possible to guide one's way to the city.

Now although Kashmir is such a marvellous paradise, this fact has been a curse to the inhabitants. Its far-famed wonders have attracted conquerors from most of the neighbouring nations, who have ruthlessly harried and trampled upon the Kashmiris, till their spirit has been broken. Only with the spread of British influence into the Punjab and northern India, during the latter part of the nineteenth century, have the people of Kashmir had a respite. This no doubt accounts for the apathy with which the Kashmiris regard the Home Rule movement in India; the memory of the terrible days of old is still far too vivid.

In order to try to raise up this hapless people, the Church Missionary Society opened a mission. The opposition of the authorities to the early missionaries was excessive, as is shown in the story of the life of the Rev. Robert Clark, the first missionary to Kashmir. However, from small beginnings things grew. At first no Europeans were allowed to remain in Kashmir during the winter; then, when the missionaries managed to get permission for permanent residence, the authorities prevented anyone from coming to see them. With difficulty a plot of ground was obtained, on which was built the beginnings of a hospital. That hospital grew, until to-day visitors to Kashmir are able to see the famous institution with which the name of the two brothers Neve will always be connected.

In 1880 educational work was started in Srinagar, with the foundation of a boys' school by the Rev. J. H. Knowles. It is of the growth and development of this branch of the Society's work, during the past fifty years, that this small book treats. From only one school in Srinagar, the work has grown until now there are four branch schools scattered through the city, which act as feeders for the central high school. At Islamabad, a town about thirty miles from Srinagar, another primary, middle and high school has been going for some years. Not only have boys been catered for, but a girls' school, started by the untiring efforts of Miss Violet Fitze, now flourishes under the vigorous guidance of Miss Mallinson.

THE RIVER FRONT, SRINAGAR CITY,

With the Mosque of Shah Hamdan in the Foreground, and the Fort on Hill in the Background

OVER-LOOKING THE CITY OF SRINAGAR

From the spire of the Shah Hamdan Mosque

SRINAGAR IN THE GRIP OF WINTER

Before launching out to follow the course of this enterprise during its eventful voyage up stream for the past fifty years, a note of explanation must be given.

One must bear in mind, while reading this narrative, that it has been up stream all the way. Those who know anything of water know that the stiffer the current the harder must the boatmen pull; slackening off means drifting down stream. This will help to explain why sometimes the methods employed may seem to have been rather severe. The only excuse that can be made to those who may feel hurt or shocked at anything that may have been done or said, is that the crew have been striving for a certain goal. To attain that goal they have employed those methods which to them seemed most suitable; results alone will show whether they acted wisely.

This is the goal which the school has before it—a goal which some day must be reached—to produce good citizens, imbued with the spirit of serving the Universal Father by following the example of Christ in serving their fellows, who will thus be able to help the people of their country to cast aside the reproach which has been put upon them by their neighbours, until they become in character a worthy complement to their most beautiful country. The *Pax Britannica* has brought 'Peace on earth' to this country; we hope that the schools may be instrumental in completing that message, so that the reign of Christ, which that message announced to the world two thousand years ago, may become an established fact in Kashmir.

There, at any rate, is the goal. It has not yet been reached by a long way; there remain many more miles for the crew to propel their craft, and who knows how strong the current may not become? All we ask of those who watch from the tow path is that they will give us their encouragement when the race is hardest, and so help us to get our 'heels well on the stretchers and drive it through.'

CHAPTER I

THE BEGINNINGS OF THINGS

ALTHOUGH the arrival of the Rev. J. Hinton Knowles in 1880 really marks the foundation of the school, the Rev. J. S. Doxey had got together five boys to whom he imparted instruction. He taught them elementary science in his own house, and also in a room set aside by Dr. Edmund Downes in the hospital. He used to take the boys for walks with him and explain to them the movements of the solar system, and at night time teach them about the stars. While supervising building operations in the hospital compound, he was able to give them practical lessons in mathematics. About two years later he left Kashmir, and the Rev. J. H. Knowles, with this nucleus, started the school.

At first opposition was very strong against the school, and all sorts of efforts were made to smash it. One of the pupils, having been seriously ill with typhoid, was of course weak from after-effects. Mr. Knowles, therefore, kindly lent this boy his own horse to ride to and from school. As soon as this fact became known tales were spread that the boy was a convert, and pressure was brought to bear upon his parents to take him away from the Mission school, while the State school offered him a post as a teacher. This boy, after being a short time in the State school, left it and returned to his old school.

At another time three old boys, now living, were imprisoned for 'learning English.' At least, that was the charge brought against them, though of course the real reason was to dissuade boys from coming to the Mission school. It is interesting to know the way these boys were caught out. A certain official became friendly with them, and finally asked them into his house, where he showed them a paper on which was some English writing; the boys read the paper and they fell into the trap. On another occasion a master with a party of boys spent a night in the lock-up; as they were leaving the polo ground one afternoon, after a game of cricket, they were seized and marched off for spoiling the turf! Only through the efforts of Mr. Knowles and Dr. Arthur Neve, through the British Resident, were they released.

Years later one of these boys, who had grown to manhood and whose sons were reading in his old school, stood out against persecution when officialdom arrayed itself with the forces of Theosophy and Mrs. Annie Besant to smash the school. Men were going round to the parents of the boys urging them to take their boys away from the Mission school, and threatening them that their boys would never get State employ if they stayed. In this way they came to this old boy, who had started a boat-building business for his living. When he was threatened with this awe-inspiring loss of career for his two sons he replied, 'That's all right, I have no intention of their going into State service, they will come into my business with me.' However this is a digression.

By 1885 opposition had so far died down that Mr. Knowles was able to leave his room in the hospital and take a separate house for his school, overlooking the river Jhelum. Five years later there was yet another move, and finally, after a third move, the school took up its present abode in a merchant's house, right in the heart of the city.

Some years later, when the Rev. C. E. Tyndale-Biscoe was in charge, pressure was brought to bear upon the three owners of the house to turn the school out. This would have been most inconvenient, so the Principal pretended that he had really been intending to turn out in any case, and let it be known that he was going round looking for another site. This, however, failed to impress the 'three wicked uncles,' as they were called, for their nephew, who is the present landlord, was then reading in the school. So the Principal thought of a plan as follows:

He felt pretty sure that the landlords were not really anxious to turn the school out, and only needed a little persuasion to allow it to remain, so that they might have an excuse to give to those who were trying to force their hand. At that time the Principal's cousin, Mr. A. B. Tyndale, and his brother-in-law, Rev. C. L'E. Burges, were helping him in the work, one with carpentry and the other, being a wrangler, with mathematics. He asked them if they would come to help him to persuade the 'three wicked uncles,' but they pleaded ignorance of the language. 'Never mind,' he said, 'simply do as I do and look as I look.'

A day was fixed for the interview between the three Englishmen and the three uncles. The Principal, with his two supporters, went round to the landlords' house. On arrival, they were told that, unfortunately, the three uncles had had to go out.

'We will see about that,' said the leader of the expedition, and, followed by the other two, he ran upstairs, and there found the 'three wicked uncles' seated on the floor. They at once got up and ordered chairs to be brought for the *sahibs*. The leader sat down, and his two friends sat down, then he began by talking pleasantly and the other two looked pleasant. However, the uncles refused to budge from their decision, so the leader began to argue and look pained, whereat the others looked pained; then he began to look stern, and then he stood up and looked angry, the others copying him in every look and action. Suddenly he thumped his fist on a table, and two other fists came, thump! thump! 'Hi diddle diddle, the cat and the fiddle, the *cow*!' he shouted, with the other two following in chorus. That was enough; at the united roar on the word 'cow!' the uncles capitulated, and besought the Principal not to move his school; they had got their excuse, and were only too glad not to lose a good let. Hence the school still stands where it did.

During the early days Mr. Knowles had started the boys on cricket, which they played, wearing all the regalia of a Kashmiri pandit of those days —tight bandage-like pugaree, golden ear- and nose-rings, wooden clogs, and the long nightgown garment, reaching from neck to ankles, called a *pheran*. This nightgown incidentally came in most useful for stopping and catching balls. Mr. Knowles also started the boys with physical exercises, and installed the parallel bars and horizontal bars. But the authorities got to hear of this, and, thinking these exercises smacked of low caste manual labour and that it was derogatory for boys of such high estate (for they were all Brahmans) to be taught such things, drilling was forbidden by order of the Maharaja.

When starting a school where opposition is strong, there are two courses open. The first is in all ways to try to conform to the wishes of the public, so as to induce them to send their sons to the school. The second course is to run the school on the lines that are considered to be the best, whether in accordance with public opinion or not; to chance the consequences of getting few pupils, but also to know that those few will get greater benefits.

Both these methods were tried in this school. In its early stages, when opposition was very great, it was run exactly like any other school in the country, the only objectionable feature being that there was compulsory Christian instruction. But even this objection did not prove so very serious, for many of the boys considered it a good opportunity for practising English, while the more prejudiced let their minds wander.

Apart from this there was little or no discipline. The Kashmiri pandit is by nature studious, he has no idea of 'ragging,' which is the cause of so many scrapes in an English school; and, as punctuality was not insisted upon, there was never any need for disciplinary action. In fact, the cursory observer might have considered them a model set of boys.

The Kashmiri boys liked lessons and hated athletics, and, since the latter were not compulsory, there was nothing in the school to rub them up the wrong way, hence no need for discipline. School was due to start at 11 a.m. as a rule, but it was seldom that all the staff had assembled before mid-day—for, going on the principle that the East hates to be hurried, it was necessary to pander to this little whim.

The boys learnt their lessons according to ancient custom: all the boys reading aloud in a monotonous sing-song, drawing in their breath with a sucking noise, just as if they were drinking soup, rocking their bodies in rhythm the while, what time the master reclined at ease at his desk.

At this time the boys (many of them being 20 years of age or more) were all Kashmiri pandits (i.e. high caste Brahmans), who all wore the regulation dress mentioned previously. The disadvantages of this dress were many. The *pheran* inhibits any violent exercise, it was commonly worn day and night for weeks, becoming dirty and a harbour for all sorts of diseases. The clogs again prevented any swift movement, also, since it was the universal custom during the winter to carry fire-pots under the *pheran*, clogs were a source of great danger, causing the wearer to trip up, while the *pheran*, which was usually worn with the arms inside, the sleeves being flung over the shoulder, served as a very useful trap to hold him down in a sort of sack-full of live charcoal. The nose-rings and ear-rings, being often very heavy and elaborate, caused sores to form, and prevented any attempt at cleaning the affected parts; pocket handkerchiefs were of course unknown. Later it will be seen how one by one these 'badges of gentility' were removed, and a more serviceable dress instituted.

Though these methods may seem very slack, and a curious way of running a school, still it must be borne in mind that things were only at the beginning, opposition was great, and it is probable that only by going slowly at first could the school have ever been started, or the public gradually educated to new ideas.

The following extracts from notes written by visitors at that time will show that they recognised the value of the school and what it stood for:

Lord Robert's, when Commander-in-Chief of India, visited the school in May, 1889, and wrote: 'Lady Roberts and myself were very favourably impressed by the appearance of the pupils generally. Mr. Knowles and the ladies who are assisting him deserve every credit for the satisfactory manner in which they are carrying on the work of education under considerable difficulties. We beg to offer him our congratulations and to express the hope that he may in time be able to extend his work throughout Kashmir.'

Col. Parry Nisbet, the British Resident in Kashmir, whom we remember on account of his determination and energy, which resulted in the building of the road into Kashmir, was a firm friend of the school in its early critical days. He writes, after a visit in 1890:

'There was a much larger attendance of pupils than I expected to see. The neat appearance and remarkable intelligence of the boys was very satisfying. The slight examination I held of several of the classes was sufficient to show that solid and valuable instruction in English, Sanskrit and Urdu is given. I trust the excellent work begun by Mr. Knowles may go on and prosper.'

When Lord Lansdowne, the Viceroy, visited Kashmir in 1891, in a speech to the school he expressed pleasure at hearing that the boys were taking to 'manly sports and exercises,' and urged the boys to copy Oxford and Cambridge, and learn to 'pull an oar, or rather work a paddle.' As will be seen in course of time, the boys learnt to take pleasure in both these sports. Lord Lansdowne made a point of warning the boys against learning 'your lessons by heart to repeat them like parrots, without considering the meaning and real drift of the words which you are learning.' In a later chapter is explained how the school tried to follow his excellent advice in this matter as well.

CHAPTER II

BREAKING UP AND BUILDING

IN Kashmir all the boats are made on much the same plan—the main difference being one of size. They are all flat-bottomed and flat-sided, like a punt, they narrow uniformly towards bow and stern, the whole hull being curved so as to lift bow and stern out of the water. A pent roof, thatched with rushes, is then put up, and one has a vessel much resembling the traditional Noah's ark. In fact, the boat builders claim that they have learnt their art from Noah. The largest of these boats are the *kutchus*, used for carrying rice and other merchandise all over the Kashmir waterways. They resemble barges, with planks some two and a half inches thick. Next in size, and more graceful to look at, are the *doongas*, used chiefly as dwelling-houses or for touring; so on down to the small *shikaras*, which ply for hire, taking the place of the rickshaws or cabs of other lands. This uniformity of plan is useful, for it means that when a *kutchu* begins to get on in years and starts leaking, it can be broken up, the rotten wood cut away, and with the remaining planks a smaller boat constructed. This in its turn is broken up, and out of its remains yet a smaller boat is made. Thus, through a series of breakings and buildings, the *kutchu* ends its days as a small *shikara*.

All those who know Kashmir will agree that these boats are perhaps the most typical features of the country. To many the Kashmiri boatmen are the only people of whom they have any vivid recollections (generally recollections of a sort uncomplimentary to the boatmen). With all their faults, however, one cannot but marvel when seeing their skill and determination in manœuvring their great unwieldy barges against the current at some awkward bend; often, too, from the stern, their better-half, steering with a great paddle, shouts caustic comments at any bad watermanship, which helps to keep them up to the mark.

Like all Kashmiris, they are gifted to a marked degree with the saving grace of humour, as the following anecdote will show:

A boatman was seen walking along the bank of the river up stream, peering into its muddy water.

'What are you doing?' said a passer by.

INCULCATING SMARTNESS

AFTER A BEGINNING HAD BEEN MADE

THE SCHOOL TO-DAY

600 BOYS AT MASS DRILL

'My wife has just fallen off that boat and disappeared, I am trying to see when she next comes up so as to save her.'

'But, surely,' said the astonished stranger, 'she will have gone down stream like everything else.'

'Not if you knew my wife.'

The reader may be asking what is the cause of this dissertation on boats in what is supposed to be the story of a school, but the connection will be seen on reading a little further.

About 1891 the policy of the school was changed, and instead of giving in to all the popular demands, it was decided to model the school on those in the West, where the authorities decide on all matters of school management and do not take their orders from the students. For example, take the matter of holidays. There were no regular school holidays, but instead innumerable gods' days and goddesses' days were given. One never could tell whether all the school, or only half, would be present on any given day; for some boys would think one god important and some another. How could there be discipline when boys could attend or stay away at their own whim? So gods' days had to go, and one by one they were suppressed by the simple expedient of fining boys who stayed away from school. In their place regular holidays were instituted, so that staff and boys could get a few consecutive weeks of rest and change, as in Western schools.

Of course, there was opposition to this change on the grounds of religion, as there always is when any innovation is introduced. But, as again, always happens when a firm line is taken, opposition dies and the terrible innovation becomes one of the unchangeable customs.

Holidays were mentioned as an example. But when once the policy of the school was changed it was evident that it was not a matter of altering or patching up, but that the whole structure would have to be broken up, the rotten part cut out, and a new healthy vessel made out of what was left—even if it meant making a great *kutchu* into a small *shikara*. It would mean pushing out of still waters into a strong opposing current, where the captain of the boat would need all his skill and determination if the vessel was not to be wrecked, and, by appealing to their quality of humour, to bring his crew along with him.

Boys were no longer canvassed to come to school, but were advised when they applied for admission to go elsewhere, or bear the consequences of coming to a school which imposed these five conditions:

(1) Compulsory Christian teaching.
(2) Compulsory games.
(3) Compulsory swimming.
(4) Compulsory fees.
(5) Corporal punishment for misbehaviour.

No other school imposed, or ever had imposed, such conditions, and yet the membership of the Mission school went up. The *kutchu* was not going to be a *shikara* after all. What was the reason for this? The reason was the same reason, ultimately, which had caused the policy of the school to be changed, The reason why the boys came was that English was taught to them by Englishmen (for by now it was no longer illegal to learn English). The reason why they wished to learn good English was to get good employ in the State, where pay was small but chances for loot great. If they could speak better English than their fathers, they could become even better looters. The policy of the school was changed because it was not considered that the result of a Mission school training should be the production of more clever scoundrels than there had been previously. So that the teaching of English brought more scholars who came for a purpose which was not desired, and that in its turn brought about a change in policy.

The policy was, somehow or other, to turn these high caste conceited Brahman sons of the ruling class into men. Men in the true and best sense of the word, who would go into State service in order to serve their State and not simply for what they would get out of it.

The rest of this story will show each phase in the struggle of putting manhood into the Kashmiris, through the past fifty years up to the ,present day.

In reading these accounts one should bear in mind that, for all their faults, the Kashmiris have good qualities, but for which the story of the school would be very different.

Mention has been made of their sense of humour. Over and over again, things have been made easier as soon as the boys had been given the gift 'of seeing themselves as others see them'; for the Kashmiris can appreciate a joke, even against themselves.

Through the centuries of oppression under ruthless conquerors which preceded the *Pax Britannica*, on account of which the Kashmiris had lost their self-respect and manhood, they had developed a wonderful cheerfulness under difficulties. Many a time, under conditions unpleasant enough to make a saint swear, the Kashmiris will start cracking jokes or singing to keep up their spirits.

Also, like that other persecuted race—the Jews—they have developed a stubbornness for their traditions. Once this stubbornness is directed towards sticking to what they know to be right and true, their allegiance to the new tradition is as firm as it was to the old.

Among the old traditions that are dying out is a strong belief in the ill-omen of sneezing. Any orthodox person who intends doing anything will desist if he should sneeze, or hear someone else sneeze. Nowadays small boys, seeing a venerable pandit of the old school coming out of his house for a walk, will go past him and sneeze; at once the old man will hurry home, to come out again a few moments later for another try. He has hardly gone a few paces before an accomplice of the first boy goes past him and sneezes. 'This is most annoying,' says the old man, as for a second time he is forced to return; so it goes on, till the last boy of the group has had his sneeze, and the old gentleman can set off on his journey with a light heart.

CHAPTER III

CLEAN OR UNCLEAN?

PRACTICALLY all the boys during the early years were Brahmans, who, being the highest caste of Hindu, are spiritually clean, and are defiled by coming in contact with all sorts of things, such as dogs and English people. Yet the nose gave distinct evidence that they were not clean. At one of the early prize days the British Resident's parting remark to the Principal was, 'Biscoe, what a dirty lot of boys you have here, I will give a prize to the cleanest boy next year.'

Their clothes have already been described, and when a boy was asked how long it was since his *pheran* had last been washed, he would often reply, 'I do not know, for it belonged to my father.' Their ear- and nose-rings prevented any proper washing of face, ears, or neck. Their finger nails were always about a quarter of an inch long (to show that they were high-born gentlemen and did no manual labour), and were always in the deepest mourning. Nearly very boy had the itch or favus, or both. Yet, if by any chance one of the European staff should touch them, they would squirm in utter disgust at such defilement. It was no use telling them that they were filthy, for they believed they were clean; so before they could become clean they had to learn they were dirty.

On one occasion the boys in a class would not allow a fellow Brahman of lower sub-caste to sit down with them. He was given a push, and landed in the lap of one of the high caste objectors. The two boys were then seized by the heads and their heads well rubbed together, so that the low caste of one went into the high caste of the other and *vice versa*. From that day to this there has never been any question of high caste, low caste, Hindu, Muhammadan, Christian, Sikh, or Parsi—all sitting together, playing together, or even boxing together.

Every day when the Principal came into the school hall, to give an address to the assembled boys who were sitting in rows on the floor, they would hastily make a path for him, lest by any chance he might, by his touch, defile their filthy clothes. He had, however, a very faithful dog, called Taffy, who would always stay where he was told. Outside the

A 50-FT. JUMP

A HEAD OF THE RIVER CREW

school hall Taffy was ordered to wait, the Principal came in, a lane was formed by the holy, he passed, the lane filled in behind him, he reached his desk, he whistled, and Taffy, the obedient dog, immediately came bounding over the assembled school to join his master. The cries, the moans, the horror and disgust were indescribable. Taffy was no respecter of persons, and day after day were they well and truly 'dogged,' till they could at last bear the touch of their Principal without a shiver.

Not only were they dirty in fact and clean in imagination, but they were utterly unmanly, while at the same time they thought themselves superior to all other creatures. They had no shame, for there were no standards of honour by which to shame them. The slave mentality had been well stamped on them by the heel of their conquerors. They had lost their self-respect, and one way to put that into them again was to make them clean instead of filthy, and smart instead of slipshod.

It was therefore with the idea of giving them self-respect that the great battle against dirt was begun.

In Kashmir there are three great enemies to cleanliness:

(1) Parents.
(2) Custom.
(3) Public opinion.

The parents say that if a boy looks clean and tidy, the devil may take a fancy to him and run off with him. Here cleanliness is not next to godliness, but just the reverse.

It was (and to a large extent is) the custom for everyone to be dirty, so that there is no standard by which they can compare themselves. Also the intense cold of the winter gives an excuse for acquiring the dirt-habit.

Public opinion, at any rate with regard to women, is that clean clothes are a sign of loose moral character.

Well, you can imagine that dirt having these three allies, strong measures had to be taken. The battle with dirt had three stages.

First, any boys who were dirtier than the average were marched off to the river bank. A rope was tied round them, and then, clothes and all, they were dipped like sheep.

Secondly, a less drastic treatment was soon enforced, for the first had succeeded in removing the first layers of dirt, so to speak. A bath tub, dog soap and a scrubbing brush were installed in the school, and the dirty boys were publicly scrubbed by the Muhammadan porter.

Thirdly, direct action was dropped, and responsibility was put upon the form masters, who must inspect their boys before lessons and send the dirty ones away to wash. If a dirty boy is subsequently found, the master is fined one rupee. We are still at this stage now, though in the summer time we have also started a campaign against dirty clothes as well as dirty bodies. We have instituted a weekly washing day during the summer, and on that day boys may come in dirty clothes and wash them after school. But if their clothes are dirty on any other day they are fined, and have to wash clothes during school hours. To a Western mind that might seem a curious punishment, but not so in the East, where boys love their books.

The itch and scald head were abolished by direct action in much the same way as the first dirt. A daily parade was held of those infected. Ointment was applied from large buckets, and well rubbed in by the European members of the staff. Now these two ailments are non-existent in the school.

CHAPTER IV

DRESS REFORM

THE school is not intended to Westernise the boys, and wherever the habits of the people are harmless or commendable, they are encouraged to preserve their national customs and dress. But wherever the customs have a harmful effect, every means is employed to try to alter them, as, for example, the custom of dirt mentioned above.

It has been asked, 'What can you expect of a people whose national costume is a night-gown?' This is the national costume of the Kashmiri; the Muhammadans wear a more serviceable variety which reaches to the knee, but the Hindu *pheran* reaches to the ankles. It is a loose garment with very long sleeves, which are often thrown over the shoulders while the arms remain underneath. A dress in which it is about as impossible for a man to do anything active as could possibly be imagined. In fact, the Kashmiris say that this dress was imposed by force upon them by Afghan conquerors in order to unman them. Men and women wear the same type of night-gown. Whether the origin of this dress is as they assert or not, the result has been achieved, and the Kashmiris continued to wear this badge of degradation of their own free will after the Afghans had gone.

Let us just once again recall the Kashmiri pandit as he was, and see how bit by bit the old costume has given place to something more serviceable, so that now he can stand up and face the world like a man.

1. Nose-ring.
2. Huge, heavy ear-rings.
3. The *pheran.*
4. Wooden clogs, for leather was pollution, so that shoes could not be worn.
5. Sixteen yards of narrow cloth, bound round the head like a bandage.

One by one these insignia of unmanliness went as follows:

The nose-ring was found to be a painful accessory when boxing was introduced. Though boxing had to wait until leather was no longer considered pollution.

Ear-rings withstood years of ridicule, but finally went when a game, called *Hi Cockaloram, jig jig jig*, was introduced. A game in which the boys on one side jump on to the backs of the other side, and have to hold on without hands while the 'horses' try to pitch them off. Holding on without hands means taking a grip with the knees, and if a pair of ear-rings is between these knees, then the ear-rings will not be there when the game is next played.

The *pheran* was replaced by trousers owing to the horizontal bar; for the boys, seeing another boy hanging head down with his one and only garment telescoped over his head, realized the humour of the situation, and decided that they, at any rate, would not be the cause of a free comedy.

Wooden clogs are hardly serviceable for playing football. Football was compulsory, 'so what can do?' Hence shoes in which a boy can walk like a boy, instead of at the sedate pace of an ox.

The tight *pugaree* was laughed at, and in its place came the graceful turban, which makes even an insignificant face take on nobility.

So we have the boy as he is to-day. A real boy, who we hope will grow into a true man. The badges of degradation are gone and the signs of self-respect are taking their place.

BOYS AND MASTERS FROM ALL THE C.M.S. SCHOOLS IN SRINAGAR, ASSEMBLED AT THE CENTRAL SCHOOL

BOYS AND FLEET OF THE C.M.S. SCHOOLS IN SRINAGAR, ASSEMBLED AT THE CENTRAL SCHOOL

CHAPTER V

HEALTHY MINDS IN HEALTHY BODIES

HAVING tackled the question of dirt and its attendant diseases, it soon became apparent that there was a far more serious disease that was undermining the boys' whole outlook, namely, disease of the mind. Boys were constantly using the foulest epithets to one another, and discussing among themselves all sorts of vice. When reproved for using some particularly filthy expression, and asked how they would like their parents to hear them using such language, they would often reply, 'Why, my mother taught it to me.'

Now this talk was merely a symptom of a disease which had much deeper roots. A disease which could only be tackled by strong measures, in fact, by the surgery of muscular action.

To show how widespread was this disease, two examples will be enough:

One day after games the boys were returning to their homes, when some hefty hooligans set on some of the smaller boys and began to beat them and carry them off. A fight ensued in which our bigger boys were victorious, and managed to capture the leader of the hooligans. In his possession they found a most illuminating book, containing the names of the president, vice-president, officers and members of the organisation to which he belonged, and also a long list of the names and addresses of good-looking boys, and a list of jackals who were willing to betray these small boys.

The facts having become known, the school did not rest there; they ran the hooligans into court, and after a great deal of difficulty had them sentenced. The judge was desirous of giving the leader seven years, but, owing to the pressure of public opinion, he had to content himself with a sentence of two years hard labour. The general public was furious at this high-handed interference with their 'sport.' But it was enough. From that day organised clubs of this sort have ceased to exist, or, at any rate, have had to carry on business more carefully.

The school did not remain idle after these hooligans had been prosecuted; but a map was put in every school,[1] with certain houses marked in red as 'cities of refuge,' where boys could run for protection. Also by various means hooligans were enticed to fall into the hands of our bigger boys and masters, who brought them to the school. Here they were able to show their pugilistic prowess before all the school, by fighting some of our best boxers instead of little boys. This usually cooled their ardour. They were always, of course, given the choice of being handed over to the police, but invariably chose our rough and ready justice. We still to this day occasionally have this form of entertainment, for though the clubs are gone, individuals often lie in wait to carry off small boys. In case anyone should be thinking that the school is able to see the depravity of the Kashmiri only, it may be mentioned that on two occasions Europeans have tried to get hold of our boys. In each case it took two years to collect the necessary evidence to have the individuals tried, convicted, and expelled from Kashmir.

The following story is a second example of the school coming up against an organisation for encouraging vice:

A group of boys were leering and smirking over a book in the school compound, and did not notice that the Principal was approaching. Suddenly one boy, who had been standing near by in evident disgust, leapt in amongst them, seized the book and handed it over to the Principal. It was a remarkable hand-painted manuscript, in which both artist and author had contrived to produce a work of the utmost bestiality.

The first thing was to know who owned the book, and a boy was pushed forward from among the crowd as being the proud possessor. The school was assembled at once, and before the whole school the owner had to eat that book (or, at least, as many ounces of it as a doctor had said he could eat without harm). He was a Brahman, and maintained that it was unclean food; but on being told that what had not been unclean for his mind could not be unclean for his body, and after other more vigorous explanations, he took his meal.

The next step was to find out where this book had come from. Enquiries showed that in a certain street of shops, owned by Brahman priests, these books were for sale. With the aid of the police these shops were raided, and their stock of 'literature' was burned.

[1] In case there should be any confusion when more than one school is indicated, it should be remembered that at first there was only the one school, later other small primary schools were opened, but, being under the same management and run on the same lines, they are really part of the original school.

The last step was to find where the books were made. Again with the help of the police, a lightning raid was made on the houses of some priests. There they were caught at their 'artistic' work, with their models posed for them, so as to get the necessary realism in their creative efforts.

Since that day no such books have entered the school, nor have they been on sale in the public bazaars.

As these two examples show, this is a very serious disease, for it has its roots in public opinion. The parents of the boys are often quite indifferent as to the moral character of their sons: it is no use going to them for help. Hence we have to make a public opinion in our school which shall be different from the public opinion of the city. We do this by punishing a boy who is caught in immorality in such a way that neither he nor the school will forget it.

This curing of diseased minds is one of the hardest surgical operations we have to tackle, and we have by no means cut out the disease as yet.

CHAPTER VI

ATHLETICS OR FLABBY GENTILITY?

AS mentioned previously, when the boys first began to do physical jerks, this was put a stop to by order of the Government. Similarly, on one occasion, after a game of cricket on the polo ground, the boys were arrested on the pretext of having spoiled the turf.

Now that was in the days of voluntary athletics, but as soon as games and drill were made compulsory the opposition came from the boys and parents, and it was a far more obstinate opposition.

There were three major reasons for opposing athletics, apart from the usual excuse which a boy always brings up as a reason against anything he dislikes, namely, that it is contrary to his religion. These three excuses were:

1. Love of books and impatience at the idea of wasting time at games which might be more profitably employed in cramming for examinations.
2. Gentility. Games bring up muscle and only manual labourers have muscle, not high-born gentlemen.
3. Leather, which being part of a dead animal is, or was, utterly unclean and untouchable. This, of course, ruled out football, boxing, and many other sports.

However, in spite of this opposition, a start was made with physical jerks, horizontal and parallel bars, and so on. The choice lying between doing these ungainly antics and leaving the school forthwith, the boys made a beginning in acquiring muscle.

The single sticks was another innovation, instituted largely to break the disgusting habit of sneaking. Boys were continually coming weeping to the Principal, with hands clasped in the attitude of prayer, the head hung over on one side and one foot rubbing the other, to tell him some tale of woe about being hit or hurt or pushed or insulted by some other boy. Could anything be more utterly without any semblance of manhood than a boy in this condition? So single sticks were used to decide these quarrels. Plaintiff and defendant were each given a stick and told to lay into one another, and behind them stood seconds with sticks to encour-

FOOTBALL

THE FIRST TEAM IN KASHMIR

SMALL BOYS PLAYING FOOTBALL

BOXING

THE OLD STYLE: 'HAMMER HIM WHEN HE IS DOWN'

THE NEW STYLE

age the boy who should all of a sudden become filled with compassion for his one-time foe. In this way they found it was better to settle their own quarrels rather than bring tales to the Principal.

Cricket they took to without much persuasion, as they saw Europeans playing it and therefore it seemed a fit entertainment for gentlemen. Also, perhaps, they were inspired by the large sums that ruling Princes pay to their professional teams. Besides which, there was no leather about it except the ball, and that can always be stopped with the *pheran* and held by means of the long sleeves of the same.

Football, however, was another story, for it meant touching leather, also running, and no gentleman may walk faster than an ox. Nevertheless, football came at last. Boys had begun to wear leather shoes, and, on being asked how they could do such a wicked thing, they said that it was not unclean provided they did not use their hands for pulling them on. Since leather was not unclean for feet, then surely football could be played. The boys, of course, were dead against it, but play they did, and the manner of their playing was thus.

On a certain morning the Principal brought a football down to school.

'What is that?' said the boys.

'A football.'

'What is it for?'

'To play with, and I am going to tell you the rules, so that we may have a game this afternoon,' said the Principal.

'What is the use of this game? Will we get any money from knowing how to play it?' the boys chorused.

'Most certainly not.'

'Then we do not wish to learn; besides is it not made of leather?'

'Yes, it is made of leather.'

'Then we may not touch it, for it is unclean.'

'What about your shoes—don't you touch them?'

'Yes, with our feet only.'

'Well, you only have to kick this with your feet.'

'No, it is different. We will not play.'

But the boys did not have the last word. With the aid of a blackboard the rules were demonstrated, and when school was over the whole lot were driven along the streets to an open piece of ground, there to have their first game.

The ball was placed in the centre, the boys ranged in their places about it, the whistle blew, but everything remained stationary. The Principal explained, 'When I blow the whistle you must kick the ball. Now then.' The whistle blew again, but the ball did not move. Again they were told, again the whistle blew and still no one moved. Then the Principal called to some men whom he had stationed near the goal posts with single sticks, in case of emergency. As soon as the pandits saw the sticks there was one concerted rush by the whole lot to see who could get nearest the ball and so avoid the stick-bearers. Not only did they kick the unholy leather, but with hands and claws they fought each other to get near it. *Pugarees* flew out like pennants, clogs and shoes shot into the air. Football had started in Kashmir.

Suddenly a terrible howl rent the air, the whole game stopped while the players began to crack their knuckles and suck their fingers and rub one foot on the other. Evidently something serious had happened for such signs of horror to be necessary.

The cause of the trouble was that one of the players had received a kiss, bang on the lips, from this unclean and utterly irreverent ball. He was allowed to be taken to a filthy canal by his comrades and there to be purified.

That was the first game. Since then football has been played regularly in the school, though in the first years boys used pins with great effect on the balls to bring the games to an end. Now, not only is football played by the school boys, but the general public have taken to it with enthusiasm. They have a football league of various teams, though all are amateur, and, as the boys were told in the beginning, they do not get any money out of football.

Of all the sports, however, the finest one for putting manhood into these products of flabby gentility was boxing. But here again progress was held up by the three great reasons—and especially, of course, leather. They might kick a leather football, but to put on leather gloves and push these parcels of defilement into each other's faces—never!

A day came, however, when one of these Brahman youths came swaggering into school with his books bound together in a natty leather satchel.

'Hallo,' said the Principal, 'what have you got under your arm?'

'Books,' the boy replied.

'Yes, I know, but what is round the books?'

'A leather case.'

'But I thought you said you could not touch leather.'

'Oh, but *Sahib*, don't you understand. This is the leather of books and that was the leather of boxing gloves.'

From that day the leather of boxing gloves and the leather of books were made of equal holiness, and the boys started on the long road of learning how to take blows without crying or losing their tempers.

Having overcome the difficulty of getting them to box, another difficulty arose. They had no self-control and easily lost their tempers. They would then throw off the gloves, and try to tear each other with their long black nails; if a boy should knock another down the correct procedure was to sit on him, and hammer him till blood was drawn.

At first when blood flowed everyone would become horrified and disgusted—for blood is another of the many defilements. Later they went all out for blood, while the onlookers stood by encouraging the stronger.

Now those days are all over. The prejudice against leather, the horror of blood, the blood lust, all are forgotten, and every day it is possible to see boys boxing with keenness, taking and receiving blows without losing their tempers. Now, instead of longing to see the weaker boy pummelled, they cheer on a boy who is putting up a plucky fight.

The opposition to boxing did not come only from Kashmir, as this remark from England will show. 'Mr. Biscoe should be told to stop teaching his boys to box, for it will only lead to prize-fighting and frequenting of public houses.' However, boxing has continued, and after twenty years there are as yet no signs of these terrible consequences. First must come the public houses, of which there are none in Kashmir, before the boys can start frequenting them.

On one occasion boxing was the means of teaching the boys that they did not know everything. Being Brahmans and sinless, they were also omniscient—even going so far as to teach the Principal how to pronounce English. So the Principal said to his would-be-teacher, who was a 'boy' of over twenty with a black beard, 'Do you know everything?'

'Yes,' said the omniscient one.

'Well, do you know how to box?'

'Yes.'

'Then, if I try and hit your nose can you prevent me?'

'Yes.'

'Right, then, we will try and see.'

Gloves were brought and the boy told to defend his nose. He was asked if he was ready, he said he was. Bang came the glove on his nose. On being asked why he had not defended his nose he said he was not ready. He pretended the laces of his gloves were not properly tied. At last he was ready, with face buried in his hands. A feint to the 'bread-basket' from the Principal brought down the hands, and again glove and nose met.

We need not follow this pantomime right through, but, suffice it to say, that at last came tears and with tears enlightenment. He did not know how to box, he could not defend his nose—in fact, he did not know everything.

For ever afterwards boxing was the talisman which had only to be mentioned, for the know-alls to admit their ignorance.

So much then for boxing, how it started, grew and flourished. The story has been much the same for all other sports or games. Some coming sooner than others.

It was not till organized games had been going for twenty-two years that boys could be brought to do the unholy thing of playing in a band. The mouth is very holy, and nothing must touch the lips except a few special things—even food must be thrown in so as to avoid the lips—hence musical instruments, such as bugles and fifes, are 'taboo.' Also only low class people are musicians.

Now every day the boys do their exercises to the strains of music, and the band is used on many other occasions as well, for instance, it gives performances in the hospitals to cheer up the sick.

Before concluding this chapter let us see why it is that we stress athletics. Is it merely to get good strong teams and win matches? That is certainly not our aim. We have no desire to encourage pot hunting in any form. None of our teams, therefore, receive special coaching. No boy can ever win a prize for winning a race or competition, for we do not wish to encourage the strong, but rather the weak.

Athletics are primarily to improve the physique of the boys. To get them into the open, for the Kashmiri boy loves 'mugging' at his books indoors, to the great detriment of his eyesight and health. Therefore, we concentrate not on the best and strongest boys—as is the temptation if match winning is the goal—but on the weakest.

Team games, such as football, help to foster *esprit de corps*, which is terribly lacking in Kashmir. Also in other sports boys can only win points for their class, instead of medals and pots for themselves. To help the weakly to take an interest, they may gain points for their school by coming to watch games, so that even if a boy can never play for his class he can contribute to its winning a challenge trophy.

Finally, athletics having built up good, strong, healthy boys, they can use their strength in helping those weaker and less fortunate than themselves. Thus through athletics we hope to raise up useful citizens, instead of first-class blood-suckers.

Before ending this chapter, an extract from a letter sent to the headquarters of the Church Missionary Society, in London, will show how strongly athletics were opposed:

'We, the inhabitants—Hindus and Muhammadans of Kashmir—want this, that if Mr. Biscoe is allowed to remain in Kashmir as a Principal of the school, not a single boy will attend it, and the Society will have to close it for good. . . . Therefore, please, sir, transfer Mr. Biscoe for he is exceedingly a bad man, illiterate, deceitful, ill-mannered, uncultured, cunning, and a man too much fond of cricket.'

CHAPTER VII

ANTIPATHY TO AQUATICS

KASHMIR is a land of water; with its broad, placid river, its network of canals and numerous lakes all inter-communicating, it is the ideal holiday place for those who love spending a summer in or on the water. There are no noxious beasts, large or small, to interfere with or harm the bather, and the clear, limpid waters of the lakes become so warm in the summer that one can remain in the water for hours without feeling cold.

Yet, in spite of all these attractions, the Kashmiris, with the exception of the professional boatmen, have an unaccountable aversion to the water. Few, even of the boatmen, know how to swim well, and practically no one in any other trade or profession.

Again the hopeless gentility of the higher castes comes in to prevent their enjoyment of the wonderful pleasure of swimming in these enchanting surroundings; for swimming is only practised by low caste boatmen. The result of this non-swimming is that the water annually takes a huge toll of lives through drowning, as when boats upset or people slip in while washing on the banks.

To combat this evil, swimming was made compulsory and a fine imposed on any boy who is unable to swim after thirteen years of age. This fine doubles each year till it becomes too expensive to be a 'gentleman.' All through the summer there is a daily swimming lesson which all non-swimmers must attend, so that now there are very few non-swimmers in the school. The result of this rule has been that our boys save anything up to thirty lives from drowning annually.

Many and curious are the devices that have been employed to evade this rule, from faking birth certificates to getting 'doctors' to write certificates saying that a boy's health does not permit him going into the water. Even fortune-tellers have been brought in, who prophesy a death by drowning if a boy goes near water. In this last case we advise the boy to learn to swim in order to avoid this fate.

One amusing case is worth recording. A boy came to the Principal for a discharge certificate, because he could not pay his fees. On enquiry,

THE DAL SWIM

READY TO SWIM THE LAKE

THE PLUNGE

THE LINE OF SWIMMERS, A MILE LONG

SWIMMING AND ITS RESULT

THE ANNUAL SWIM ACROSS THE DAL LAKE

A GROUP WHO SAVED LIFE FROM DROWNING DURING ONE YEAR

it was found that his fees had increased fourfold because he would not swim, as his father had ordered him not to swim.

The Principal wrote out the discharge certificate with great eagerness, as he said he was glad to get rid of such a fool. Just as the boy was leaving his study he called him back, and said, 'Tell your father from me that I hope you will die by drowning. Now you may go.'

Again the boy reached the door, and was again recalled, and had this further message to deliver: 'Tell your father that I hope he, too, will die by drowning.'

Within twenty minutes the father arrived at the school, and, putting his hands together in the attitude of prayer, asked for his boy to be readmitted, and even consented to his learning to swim if only the terrible curse should be removed.

Besides the indignity attached to swimming, the Kashmiris believed that the lakes and waters were inhabited by malign spirits, who would certainly pull you under even if you could swim. Especially is the Wular Lake, at the end of the valley, dreaded because of its ghostly inhabitants.

The boys have by learning to swim laid these ghosts. First the Dal Lake, near Srinagar, was freed, by a party of boys swimming across it. Now each year about a hundred boys do the four miles' swim, and show real keenness about it. Then the people said that it was at night that the goblins were most potent, so a midnight swim across the Dal cleared this lake of its nocturnal terrors. The Wular Lake, however, was a harder problem, and it was many years before a party of boys could be persuaded to attempt to swim across its five miles of water. Of this party no boy succeeded in crossing, for a little bit of weed or floating driftwood would touch a toe, and immediately the boy thought the goblins had got him. In the end, however, after some years, not only did parties of boys swim across, but the inhabitants of the shores of the Wular saw the advantage of learning to swim, and joined our boys in their annual swim.

On one occasion the boys were able to kill a 'crocodile,' which had somehow got into the river, to the great fear of all the inhabitants of Srinagar, so that for a whole month they were prevented from bathing.

One summer's day a pandit was doing his ceremonial washing on the river bank, when his foot slipped and he sat down heavily on a piece of broken pottery. He hastily got up, and began to head for home with blood dripping from the gash in his seat. Those standing near, seeing this, began to say, 'Did you see that blood? Perhaps a fish has bitten him. What fish could it be, for Kashmir fish never bite? Perhaps it was a crocodile!' Thus came the crocodile, and before it finally died it had killed and maimed hundreds of people.

In order to kill this crocodile, so that the citizens might wash and follow their lawful occasions on the river bank in peace, volunteers were called for from the school. One hundred boys volunteered. One hundred boys entered the river at the first bridge of the city, while crowds anxiously watched them from the bridge and banks of the river; however, one hundred boys got out again three miles lower down, at the seventh bridge. The crocodile was dead.

From swimming let us turn to boating. The first form of boating which the boys took up was rowing, and this is how it came about.

One morning a young Englishman, who had recently joined the staff, rowed himself down to school, instead of coming in state in a Kashmiri *shikara*, propelled by boatmen. The boys and masters, seeing this amazing sight, put their heads out of the windows and said, '*Coolie Sahib! Coolie Sahib!*'

'Right,' said the young man to himself, 'but there will be some coolie Brahmans in Kashmir before to-day is over.'

On arrival in the school hall he picked out two strong young masters and said, 'Come along with me, I am going to teach you how to row.'

'No,' they said, 'we cannot do such a thing, for it will give us muscle; also there is leather on the oars.'

However, muscle or no muscle, leather or no leather, they were herded down the passages and stairs, till they stood on the landing below which the boat was tied. A push from behind landed them safely, though a trifle ruffled, in the bottom of the boat. The young Englishman jumped in behind them, untied the painter, and away they drifted on the current. The Englishman took up his position in the stern, while the two sullen pandits faced him.

'Now then,' he said, 'you will have to row, for you will never reach land again except by your own efforts.'

Slowly they drifted down, turning round and round.

'You had better make up your minds soon,' said the *Coolie Sahib*, 'for the further we drift the further you will have to row, and if you have never rowed before you will get blistered and find it excessively painful.'

At last, after they had drifted like this under three of the city bridges,

ROWING

THE FIRST KASHMIRI OARSMEN

THE 12-OARED CUTTER, MANNED BY MASTERS

PADDLING

THE FIRST CREW OF BRAHMANS WHO DARED TO PADDLE

BOATS CREWS OF THE PRESENT DAY

they saw the game was hopeless. So, taking the oars, they managed to row the boat back to school. The trick was done, and from that day many hundreds of high caste Brahmans have learnt the joy of swinging together.

When it came to paddling a boat like a Kashmiri boatman, it was quite another matter. What *Sahibs*, albeit *Coolie Sahibs*, can do, Brahmans perhaps may do without too much loss of face; but paddling like an ordinary low caste boatman, that was unthinkable. Nevertheless, within four years from the time that they first rowed, a crew of thirteen Brahmans, brave enough to face public opinion, paddled a boat right through the city.

The banks of the river and the bridges were crowded with a hooting, jeering mob, come to curse these degraders of Brahmanism. The crew looked like some obscure order of monks, or a branch of the Ku Klux Klan, for every member had completely hidden himself under a blanket. The cox had left just a chink to see through. This was in order that their identity should not be discovered, and so bring trouble on themselves and their families!

Shortly after this, when paddling had become an established fact, it happened that a crew were out for a practice paddle with a young master coxing.

As they paddled along they met H.H. the Maharaja Pratap Singh out for an airing in his State barge, with thirty paddlers. The master at once gave the order, 'Salute His Highness the Maharajah Bahadur.' Immediately all the crew stood up, holding their paddles aloft, while the young master stood smartly to attention.

'What is the meaning of this?' said His Highness with interest, as he had never seen Brahmans propelling a boat before.

'This is physical exercise, Your Highness,' said the master.

Now, as he said this, the boat, having no one to steer it, collided with His Highness' boat with a sharp bang, over went the master backwards into the water.

'Look!' said His Highness to his courtiers, 'that is physical exercise.'

Now, on every Tuesday afternoon all through the summer, boat-loads of boys may be seen racing together, Kashmiri fashion, and loving it. The end of these regattas is always marked by the whole fleet sinking. The crews stand up, rush to the bows of their boats as the boats are moving. The noses dip under, and down the whole lot go. The boats have to be turned turtle, righted, baled out, and paddled to the winning post.

This weekly practice has been the cause of saving life on many occasions, when our boys, or old boys, have been in a boat which has capsized; for they have known exactly what to do, and so saved the other passengers who were struggling wildly.

Finally, the last form of aquatics to which the boys have been introduced is sailing. Every Easter holidays a party of boys and masters, especially those with a tendency to phthisis, row down to the Wular Lake to spend a week in camp, where they are able to learn how to use the winds of the Wular for their enjoyment.

As mentioned above, the Wular is terribly dreaded, and rightly so, because of the sudden fierce storms which descend upon it. Being about fourteen miles by seven, fairly big waves get up, and the flat-bottomed Kashmiri boats do not stand a chance if caught far from land in one of these squalls.

When the Wular trip was first suggested, no single master or boy would come without the threat of expulsion from the school. Imagine such a thing in an English school, the offer of a week's holiday, sailing and boating, with all expenses paid, only accepted under compulsion!

The first time the boys found the boat moving by sail and without visible propulsion, they felt sure the hobgoblins had seized the boat and were dragging it to certain destruction, and they began to whimper and weep. Those who had food with them began to throw it overboard to propitiate the demons, others began to pray and offer the gods much rice, sugar, and milk, if they granted them a safe return.

Similar to the fear of the Wular was the fear of the mountains. No one ever climbed mountains, except one or two which were places of pilgrimage, for the mountains were feared as the home of the gods.

It was from one of the Wular camps that the boys, accompanied by the Principal and his brother, were first persuaded to climb a mountain. The boys were in fear and trepidation the whole way up, lest they should meet the gods; while the Principal urged them on, for he said he would like to catch sight of a god, as he had never seen one.

On reaching the summit, having met no gods on the way, they found a large rock. Obviously the gods were hiding behind the rock. The party was accordingly divided into two groups, one to go with the Principal one way, while the other group, under his brother, should go the other way. They would thus outwit and entrap the gods.

THE WULAR LAKE. (INSET, THE FIRST KASHMIRI TO SWIM ACROSS.)

A SAILING PARTY RETURNING AT EVENING, AFTER A DAY'S OUTING ON THE WULAR LAKE

THE WULAR SWIM

OILING BEFORE TAKING TO THE WATER

READY TO JUMP IN AND SWIM TO THE FAR SHORE, SEEN IN THE BACKGROUND

The two groups set off in opposite directions. As the boys very cautiously crept round the rock, they began to hear sounds. 'What was that?' they whispered to each other. 'Surely there is someone talking round the corner!' they said, as they got further.

'Go on,' said the Principal, 'we are most certainly going to catch some gods.'

At last the boys turned the fateful corner, and then fell into the arms of their equally terrified companions, who had gone round the other side.

'Why, sir,' said one of the boys, when he had got over his relief at finding boys instead of gods, 'why, sir, the tops of the mountains are just like the bottoms.'

Since that day the boys have gone many mountain trips. In fact, nowadays they are continually asking that expeditions may be arranged on holidays and weekends, even going so far as to pay their own expenses.

Many are the tales of the Wular, of the storms which have been weathered, of the journeys across the lake after a long expedition, when night had overtaken them and there was no light by which to guide the boat.

Gradually, little by little, the demons of wind and water, and the powers of darkness and fear, were overcome, till nowadays there is eagerness to be numbered among the 'Wular horses,' and the boys whistle for the wind on calm days.

A whole book could be written about the yarns of the Wular. Yarns, full of thrills in the sudden storms, of long expeditions when the Kashmiri spirit of cheerfulness has stood them in good stead, and through all the yarns runs the silver thread of humour.

Space, however, permits only the mention of one or two.

The party had made an expedition across the lake and were thinking of returning in the evening, when great black storm clouds began to gather. The villagers begged them not to set out, as they said it was certain death to venture in such a storm as was gathering. This was true, for a Kashmiri boat could never have weathered it. However, the Principal was determined to go, so, setting their sails, away they went for a long ten-mile run over angry water, bang into the oncoming storm. The villagers watched the little boat disappear into the thick black cloud and appear no more. Later on, an oar and some boat gear was washed up on the beach, and they thought that their worst fears were realised.

The local magistrate was informed that Mr. Biscoe and a party of boys had perished in the storm. Within a few hours the news, telegraphed up to Srinagar, was all over the city.

Next day the party who had set sail so rashly heard vivid tales of their own death.

The little boat had weathered the storm, as many before and after, and had reached the camp long after dark, when all the others had gone to bed, never thinking that the boat would attempt to come home in such a storm.

It is during these expeditions on the Wular and the mountains that the Kashmiri spirit of cheerfulness comes out with remarkable effect.

How often have the boys put on a cheerful countenance, at times when the more impatient Westerner would be swearing at the weather and losing his temper with his companions.

Many a time, when cold and hungry, with many miles to walk or row in the pouring rain, before they can reach shelter, warmth and refreshment, the humorist of the party will set them all laughing, so that troubles are forgotten and the long weary miles become somehow magically shortened.

Here is one example of their fortitude. One night a terrific storm suddenly descended on the camp, tents were torn from their pegs, and the occupants rudely awakened to find deluges of rain descending upon them. The Principal hastily got out of his houseboat to see how the camp was faring.

Guided by the brilliant flashes of lightning, he worked his way towards where the camp should be; as he approached he heard, through the rumblings of thunder, the sound of music.

Having reached the spot whence the music came, he found all the camp huddled within one tent, which had withstood the first blast, though even through this there poured a miniature river. There they all were, singing away, while they hung on to the tent pole for dear life to prevent their one remaining shelter from going the way of the rest.

What then is the object of all this boating? Again, as in athletics, to help to build up strong, useful citizens. Also that they may learn to enjoy and love the water, instead of dreading it and looking upon watermanship with contempt. But beyond all this, that they may use their watermanship in helping their fellow citizens.

As has been mentioned, they are able through their knowledge of swimming to save many lives from drowning, also on many occasions where boats have got into difficulties they have been able to put matters right. During flood time, when no one except skilled boatmen dare put out on the swirling waters, and even at times when boatmen are afraid, they are able to save countless lives and much property.

Incidentally, the boatmen do not love them on such occasions, because the boatmen look to floods to give them a rich harvest; for they can put up their prices when a man is bargaining for his life. It is then that our boys can come in and carry off the boatmen's prey to a place of safety.

Besides all these ways of helping, the boys carry annually many hundreds of convalescents from the hospitals for joy-rides in their boats on the river and lakes, to cheer up their spirits and help their recovery.

CHAPTER VIII

OF THE READING OF BOOKS THERE IS NO END

THE reader will no doubt be asking whether the boys do any studies in this school, as they have been so little mentioned. The answer is that they do the usual subjects in much the same way as in most schools, and the reason that they have received such small attention is that Kashmiri boys so love their lessons that there is very little effort required to keep them up to the mark in this line. Also the average intelligence of the Kashmiri is remarkably high, and bookwork does not have to be drubbed into him.

However, in various ways, the boys' outlook on life has had to be altered in this as in other lines.

Firstly, their object in learning was not to acquire knowledge, nor from any desire to broaden their minds, but because they wished to pass examinations. This goal attained, the way lay open to Government service and a 'cushy' job. This outlook had to be altered somehow.

Secondly (as has been said), they knew everything there was to know and only came to the Mission school to perfect their English by talking with Englishmen. All other teaching was either false or irrelevant. Only those who have seen it know what we mean by the 'pandit eye.' In early days many of the boys would look at their teachers through eyes in which were the profoundest contempt mixed with cunning, and yet in the look was also cowardice. They used to boast that they were cowards, and that their fathers were cowards, and that it was a good thing to be cowardly.

With mouths drooping open and noses screwed up so as to draw the lips into a sneer, the scholars used to face their teacher. A hopeless state of affairs, it seemed; yet to-day the 'pandit eye' is a rarity, and when found it is not long before we give the possessor a new pair of eyes.

Their knowledge was universal, for instance, the earth was flat and the sea made of melted butter. It was no good telling them otherwise, for they knew that they were right. Even the masters believed these 'facts.'

In one examination the boys were asked, 'What is the shape of the earth?' and one clever boy, in order to score marks and also to salve his conscience, wrote, 'The earth is round (so Mr. Biscoe says).'

INHALING FRESH AIR WHILE IMBIBING KNOWLEDGE

CLASSES OUT OF DOORS

AN EXAMINATION IN PROGRESS

THE SCHOOL ASSEMBLED ON A HILL, 1,000 FT. ABOVE THE CITY TO LEARN THE GEOGRAPHY OF THEIR OWN COUNTRY

In order to get them to believe that the sea was made of salt water, a party of masters had to be sent to Karachi, with orders to take ship to Bombay, in order that they might see, feel, and taste the sea. Those masters had also to visit Ceylon to see that the British did rule it, for no Kashmiri Brahman believed that. Their argument was, 'Ceylon is the home of the gods, and who are the British to dispossess them?' When the masters returned and admitted that the sea was made of salt water, the priests said to them, 'You evidently never went to the sea, for if you had you would have found that we were right, and that it was made of melted butter.' However, bit by bit the boys began to change. They ceased to be 'know-alls' through boxing, as has been explained, and they came to believe in the world as it really is. But they were unable to comprehend the expanse of the sea. In drawing maps they continually wrote names of towns miles out to sea. To counteract this, and give them an idea that the sea was water, a start was made near home. A raised map of their city was made on glass. They knew that glass represented water. Later a larger scale map of the district round was made, showing the lakes, and again where glass showed they knew it was water. Finally, maps of different parts of the world were shown, and they realised that the glass was water.

Most of the boys had never left Kashmir, and many had not even been out of Srinagar. How could one hope to explain things to them when they had no standards by which to judge? So pictures were collected. All sorts of pictures, from post cards to posters, and they began to learn through the eye. Now every room in the school represents a country, and the pictures of that country are on the walls, and the boys live in that country for a year. Our hope is that at the end of that time they may know something about that country.

One of our most difficult problems is combating the unhealthy habit of cramming for the public examinations of the Panjab University. Passing of examinations kills all desire to learn of anything outside the syllabus. Provided you pass, it does not matter by what means, or whether you know anything thoroughly or not. Examinations of this kind put a premium on cheating and on parrot mentality, and are a terrible handicap to the advance of true education. If a boy is caught cribbing by us, he is made to bring his books into all the remaining examinations, and he must get the whole paper absolutely right. He then gets nought for the examination, and is consequently put down one class. We have to be very severe with regard to this offence, as the Kashmiri thinks it no disgrace. Also we want our boys to love knowledge and not examination passes. We want wise owls and not clever parrots, like those whose screechings and screamings in India to-day out-rival wireless in the distance their noise carries, and also in the amount of attention that people pay to them.

What we are after is the 'wise old owl who sat in an oak, the more he heard the less he spoke. The less he spoke the more he heard. Was he not a wise old bird?'

In years gone by there was an annual prize distribution, and all the clever boys who were top of their classes came forward to receive handsomely bound volumes. This, thank God, is now gone.

Individual prizes put a premium on cribbing. They also reward the boys who have already received their reward, because they have been gifted with brains.

We wish to help the dull and stupid boy, and we do not wish to encourage any natural ability for cheating. Therefore, we now give no individual prizes whatever, in work any more than games. We do, however, give a prize to that class which gets the highest average of marks in the year; thus it is in the interest of the clever boys in a class to help the dull ones; it may cause a class to lose the prize if a boy lowers the average by cribbing; and the master is saved a lot of trouble, for the class will deal with slackers.

Over and above all these methods of trying to instill a love of knowledge, we also insist on boys learning about things of general usefulness, such as the Panjab University does not consider of any importance. All these items are lumped together under general knowledge, and consist of the following:

1. A knowledge of the geography of their own country of Kashmir, and especially of their city of Srinagar. A boy will willingly learn all there is to know about Melbourne, San Francisco or Leeds, if the Panjab University requires it; but will be incapable of telling you how to get from one part of his own city to another, or of naming the products of Kashmir. We think differently.

2. A knowledge of the different kinds of boats, houses, agricultural implements, etc., which are in his own country. This is to try to make him use his eyes and intelligence.

3. A knowledge of the differences between the common birds, their habits, food, etc. Also to be able to distinguish the common trees by their

leaves and to know their uses. This is to try to get them to use their eyes, to go in for nature study, to have hobbies, instead of fugging indoors, swotting all their spare time; and also that they may get interested in animals. Interest in animals leads to helping them when they are in trouble.

4. A knowledge of everyday events that are taking place in the world around them. This will take their eyes away from the narrow limits of Kashmir, and help them to realise something of the vastness and variety of the world. By learning of other countries they may learn to appreciate the beauties of their own, to which many are at present quite blind; also we hope to inspire in them a true love of their country, so that they may give their lives to its faithful service and turn their eyes from loot to something higher.

This modern history is also useful to the boys, as it enables them to contradict authoritatively the poisonous lies that certain would-be 'future rulers' love to spread around the city, about 'British atrocities on the enslaved peoples of India.'

All this general knowledge is imparted as far as possible by eye; pictures, illustrated papers and models are used; also once a week a résumé of the week's news is given to the staff, and they pass it on to the boys.

One of the staff has become keenly interested in natural history, and the boys are at last beginning to be inspired by him. We also have a library for the boys, besides one for the staff, in which are all sorts of books of travel. The Kashmiris look on reading fiction as a waste of time, and cannot understand why we wish to read of something which never happened. The boys have hardly ever taken advantage of their library. In spite of our efforts, general knowledge is still looked upon as unnecessary, for it does not help them with their examinations; we have, in consequence, to use strong measures.

If a class does badly in this subject evidently the master has not been doing his job, and is punished accordingly. But if one or two boys do badly or absent themselves from the examination, they are not promoted in class at the end of the year. This keeps the clever parrots up to the mark, for general knowledge cannot be crammed like their other subjects. It depends entirely on a boy keeping his eyes open and his intelligence alert.

CHAPTER IX

HONEST LABOUR IS WORSHIP

MANY boys are quite incapable of ever succeeding in the scholastic line, and this is true of the Brahman youths as much as any other. Yet by immemorial custom the only work open to a Brahman was pen-pushing, and any form of artizanship was impossible without loss of caste.

After some years one or two boys, who were utterly hopeless at books, though quite intelligent in other directions, had been persuaded to take up other professions instead of wasting time trying to pass examinations in order to acquire clerkships. The first Brahman boy to take up a menial job (for all jobs except clerkships are menial) had to face a considerable amount of bullying. Among other things, for instance, nobody would give him a daughter in marriage.

In the year 1899 Mr. A. B. Tyndale came out to help in the school, and, being a first-class carpenter, he started a workshop for those boys who, it was considered, would never succeed in examinations. It was a difficult job to get this work going, for, besides the inherent disgrace attached to it, the pandit, through generations of neglect, had completely lost the art of using his fingers, except for pen-pushing. This is a remarkable thing, when one considers the wonderful masterpieces of intricate workmanship in wood-carving, painting and embroidery, etc., which the Muhammadan craftsmen turn out.

When the workshop was first started, it was a certainty that any tool which a Brahman boy used would be smashed during the lesson. The first thing, then, was to give them something very simple, in which they could not do much damage.

One would suppose that anyone could hammer back and pull out nails from some old planks. This was the job on which the first Brahman carpenter was set. At the end of an hour or so, one nail had with great labour been extracted and the plank smashed to smithereens.

It is hardly conceivable, but this 'know-all,' having been shown exactly how to take out nails (' first hammer the nail back through its hole, then seize the head and draw it back with the pincers '), had thought he knew better.

MANUAL LABOUR

AN EARLY ATTEMPT AT A CARPENTRY CLASS

ISLAMABAD BOYS CARRYING MATERIALS FOR CONSTRUCTING NEW SCHOOL BUILDINGS

MANUAL LABOUR

CLEANING OUT A TANK

ROCK SHIFTING

He argued that, 'the nail is protruding so far through this side, it seems a pity to waste it,' so, seizing it with the pincers, he tried to pull the head through the wood. Naturally this needed a lot of strength, took a lot of time, and split the plank.

Once again he was shown the right way of doing the job. He was carefully shown that a large head will not go through a small hole, and left to take out some more nails.

On his teacher's return, a short time later, he saw a terrific tussle going on, as the boy tried to pull the nail the wrong way through the plank. He knew best.

As it was with nails, so with everything else. However, Mr. Tyndale carried on, he saw his tools smashed, he even found that his grateful pupils would carry off and steal his tools if he did not keep a sharp look-out, but he stuck to it, until after two years he had turned out one or two first-class carpenters. He never passed anything but perfect work, for the Kashmiri is inclined to be slipshod, and take as his motto, 'It will do.' Many a time a ricketty chair would be brought with pride to Mr. Tyndale by its maker. It would be examined, found wanting, and smashed up, and the disconsolate pupil told to go and have another try.

Unfortunately, owing to ill-health, Mr. Tyndale had to leave Kashmir and his work ceased, for there was no one else to teach this craft; for no Muhammadan carpenter was willing to let out the secrets of his trade to Brahmans.

There are still one or two of those early carpenters doing excellent business as the result of what they learnt; and, because of the strictness of Mr. Tyndale in never allowing slipshod work to past, these carpenters draw excellent pay, for one can rely on their work being sound right through. One of these early carpenters was making about Rs. 30 a month, but because he was doing manual work no one would give him a daughter for his wife. So he gave up carpentry and took a job as a *chaprasi* on Rs. 12, and at once a bride was forthcoming.

Some years later another attempt was made to get the boys to learn carpentering, under the Muhammadan school carpenter, but this withered away after a short time.

Now at last one of our Brahman masters, who has learnt carpentry, basket-work and book-binding, runs a regular technical school. While another of our old boys, who has had himself trained as a mechanic, runs a smithy, where boys can learn to be blacksmiths, motor mechanics and electricians.

We have made it compulsory for all junior masters to take lessons in the technical department, so that they can teach their boys. We have more boys applying than we have teachers who are proficient—so things are changing.

The cause of this change is not far to seek. The money value of pass Matriculation, or even F.A., B.A., and M.A., of the Panjab University is falling. An examination pass is no longer the talisman for a clerkship. Each year the schools and colleges turn out so many hundreds of examination passes, and there are only a few dozen clerkships for which this crowd has to scramble.

The public are at last realising this, and are therefore not so averse to their sons having a second string to their bow. Also, whereas in early days all the boys in the school were Brahmans who despised manual labour, nowadays half the boys are Muhammadans who have a better idea of the dignity of labour.

On our workshop we have written, 'Honest Labour Is Worship,' for we wish the boys to realise that true worship, namely, the service of God, is honest labour, and that a religious pen-pusher who practises graft is not among the true worshippers, in spite of all his religion.

We wish the boys to realise that they serve God by doing an honest day's manual labour, far better than by loafing around and living on others while waiting for a clerkship to turn up—whatever public opinion may have to say about Brahmans offending the gods by doing coolie work.

CHAPTER X

TO MAKE THE PUNISHMENT FIT THE CRIME

IN the early days, when the boys never had to do anything which they did not like, of course there was no need of punishments. But as soon as unpleasant duties had to be done then things began to happen.

We all know the ordinary punishments so common in English schools, namely, writing pages of lines or the cane. Now both these forms of punishment have obvious disadvantages, and by their frequent use they cease to have any deterrent effect. In fact, a boy who undergoes punishment becomes almost a hero, so that boys will court punishment.

In this school, in Kashmir, lines have been abolished and the cane is looked upon as a surgeon's knife, only to be used when other methods fail. As the surgeon does not wish to use his knife twice for the same operation, so here the same attempt is made to limit the use of the cane, in order that it shall be curative rather than merely a temporary measure.

Of all punishments, the Kashmiri hates ridicule most, and we therefore try so to punish a boy that the school will see him as a fool, and by laughing at him make him see himself a fool; thus he may be preserved from growing into a bigger fool. We wish to have the boys on our side when we punish—not with the culprit. We wish them to realise that he has sinned against the community, and is not to be pitied or honoured.

Another thing we have to bear in mind in dealing with Kashmiris is that, if a boy is once thoroughly punished for an offence, there is every chance of his turning out a first-class citizen; but if he be let off a punishment he deserves, or receives a mild punishment, then trouble will follow.

In this connection we have absolutely refused to grant boys scholarships, for every boy who has been helped by the school and taken in free has gone to the bad, and become an enemy of the school. This is the result of the same mentality which trades on kindness when punishment is excused. If, however, a class choose to subscribe and support a poor boy, they may do so. The boys know better than we do whether the one they support is worth it. The class usually makes the boys they support do odd jobs for them, such as tidying their classrooms, etc. This system helps the class to be generous, and gives the poor boy his education without spoiling him.

But to return to punishments. We always try to make the punishment fit the crime—that is, if a boy has done something he should not, he must go on doing it in public till he is sick of it. For instance, boys who argue or talk too much have to stand on a perch, called the parrot perch—there they must talk. They may talk about anything they like, they may revile their masters if they choose, provided they keep on talking. A school porter standing below sees to it that conversation does not flag. The parrot perch can accommodate three parrots.

A similar punishment for dirty tricks is the monkey pole, where the dirty tricks can be performed in full view of the public. For the 'pandit eye,' for liars and conceited fellows, we have two large mirrors, so placed that a boy can see both his front view and back view at once. Here the 'pandit eye' can stare at its equal. The liar can tell lies and receive them, or the conoeited fellow may meet an equally eminent personage. They simply stand and stare at their own image until they see themselves as others see them.

There are no rules in the school except one: 'Behave as a gentleman.' Rules are a weariness and only penalise the innocent: for rules are often made lest an unscrupulous boy should take advantage of freedom; thus the innocent suffer, for they lose a harmless pleasure. Also with rules often goes an unwritten but well understood scale of penalties. A boy can easily calculate whether it is worth while to take the risk.

By our system the boy with a conscience is not penalised, whereas any boy who does not behave as a gentleman gets something. He can never calculate what that something will be. This system also catches that irritating person who always just manages to keep within the letter of the law.

Mention has been made of our punishment with regard to cribbing, which will be seen to conform with this system.

One or two stories, however, are worth mentioning before closing this painful chapter.

In every class there is a money box, and the classes compete with one another to see which can give most in charity each month. This system has been in vogue for many years, to try and get the Kashmiri boy to turn

THE WEEKLY REGATTA ON THE DAL LAKE

BOYS SWIMMING THROUGH THE CITY TO KILL THE CROCODILE. (See page 24)

his hand palm downwards. Many years ago the Principal came down to school one day, on the first of the month, intending to open the money boxes in each classroom and declare the result to the assembled boys.

He found, however, that someone else had got in first, and every single box was open and empty. He at once ordered the school gates to be closed and every boy searched. One boy was found with seventy-six small copper coins in his possession. It was unlikely that he was in the habit of carrying such a mass of loose change; also the boys never gave anything in charity except small coppers, so that everything pointed to him as the thief. The boy, realising he was caught, eventually confessed.

The punishment was made to fit the crime. A blacksmith was called in, and ordered to fashion a collar out of the coins, to fit the boy's neck. The collar was engraved with a suitable inscription, and he had to wear it for seventy-six days—one day for each coin. Though this boy never stole again at school, the last that was heard of him was years after, when he stole the money of a friend who was paying him a visit. So the punishment evidently was not quite enough in his case.

Here is an example of the result of letting a boy off his punishment. A fine boy, who held a very high place all-round in the school, being captain of football and boating and also very keen on social service, went wrong morally with some other boys, and was caught out. On the day fixed for the punishment the school was assembled, and the boys who were to be punished were called up in turn to take their choice of punishment.

Because the boy in question had been a great leader in the school, his punishment was to be harder in that he had to wait till last. He watched the others go up before him and make their choice. Then his turn came, he was utterly ashamed of himself if ever a boy was, and could not raise his head. He stood before the Principal, and was asked the same question as the other boys. Without looking up he said, 'I will take both punishments.' Surely if ever there was a chance to forgive a Kashmiri, it was this. Never before had a boy shown so clearly that he was ashamed of himself, or asked that his shame should be made known publicly—for that was the alternative punishment. Anyhow he was forgiven the whole punishment, whereupon he fell down in a dead faint. From that day he did all he could to smash the school. When playing full-back at football against other schools, he deliberately let the ball pass him. He finally left and went to another school, and persuaded some of our best paddlers to desert with him, and in the following year had the honour of defeating his old school in a boat race by cheating.

The last story of this chapter shows how a boy nullified his punishment by his sense of humour.

For some offence a boy was ordered to duck himself in the river on a winter's day. Without waiting to take off his clothes, he immediately jumped in, wearing an overcoat, and started to swim around. When told that he might come out again and get warm and dry, he continued calmly swimming about, and with a broad smile said, 'Thank you very much, sir, but I am enjoying this.'

CHAPTER XI

THE STAFF

ANY account of the school would be incomplete without some knowledge of the staff by whose efforts so much has been done to propel the schools for fifty years against the stream.

In the early days, of course, it was impossible to bring in any changes, for the staff were of the old order, and loved things to remain as they were in the beginning, for ever and a day. There was very little to choose between the staff and boys in the matter of cleanliness, disease, odd ideas about the nature of the world, or the more serious matters of honour and morality.

Slowly, however, the upholders of the old order went and were replaced by old boys of the school who had been brought up in the new way of thinking, and were willing to do their utmost to break with what was bad in the past.

Now practically every member of the staff is an old boy, and it is owing to this that the school runs on oiled wheels. Every master has to be a drill instructor, he has to attend games to see that the boys are playing, and, above all, each master is the tutor of about twenty-five boys, whom he must get to know thoroughly, by visiting them at home and by watching the kind of company they keep out of school. It is through the example of the masters that the boys are encouraged to go out to do all sorts of jobs of social service where wanted.

The masters have a pretty busy life, for their work is by no means over with the closing of the classroom door.

Every day the boys leave school down shoots and poles, as a sort of fire drill. Now it is often terrifying for small boys to do this, so that the masters are supposed to show them the way. It was noticed that some of the small boys were funking the highest forty-foot pole. Enquiry showed that the master in charge had never been down the pole himself, but tried to force the boys down with threats. His penalty was to go down the pole one hundred times before the Principal should see his face again.

Next day the Principal saw him at school and asked what he was doing there? 'Oh,' said the headmaster, 'I told him to come here at six o'clock this morning, and he just finished his hundredth slide before school opened. But will you please excuse him from duty to-day, as he is very stiff and sore?' Since then that master has always been the first to descend this particular pole.

The reason for installing these poles was in order that the school could be emptied quickly in case of earthquakes, which are of frequent occurrence in Kashmir. On one occasion, before the poles had been put up, there was a rather severe earthquake shock and there was nearly a tragedy. A certain highly educated gentleman, who had come up from India to join the staff, was so keen to save his precious body that he made a bolt for the door, forgetting the scripture lesson he was giving at the time. This caused a panic among the boys, and they all began to scramble over the desks to fight their way out.

Talking of this precious gentleman, one might mention that many people have criticised the school on account of its being staffed mainly with Hindu and Muhammadan Kashmiri masters. Many a time gentlemen have been imported from India to fill this deficiency, but few have remained, for the example these teachers of scripture have set the boys has certainly not been such as would lead the boys to accept the religion which they preach without practising. Whereas, many of the Kashmiri staff practise this religion without preaching it. We do not often succeed in getting it both ways.

The commonest, though by no means the worst, fault of these imported gentlemen is the disease of wind in the head. So many men suffering from this disease had been tried, that on one occasion the following advertisement was inserted in the papers: 'Wanted, a Christian headmaster for the C.M.S. High School, in Kashmir. No man with proud look or high stomach need apply.'

This advertisement caused quite a sensation at the time in babu circles; albeit the applicants, of whom there were over seventy, in answering the advertisement were most careful to mention the mildness of their look and lowness of their stomach.

Turning from these gentlemen, and once more considering our staff, this amusing story will show that one must not always believe what one hears or even what one sees. It was about the time when the campaign was going on against gods' days, that on one of these holy days a master was

THE STAFF AND BAND

Upper Verandah, from left to right:
Standing—Shenker Koul (Headmaster), Rev. J. S. Dugdale, Miss M. Mallinson, Miss Mosse, Miss Ahmad Shah, Rev. and Mrs. C. E. Tyndale-Biscoe.
Seated—Miss H. L'E. Burges, Mrs. J. S. Dugdale, S. W. Steane, Esq.
Lower Verandah, at the back: E. D. Tyndale-Biscoe, Esq.

SOME OF THE HELMSMEN

THE HEADMASTER, SHENKER KOUL, ENTERED THE SCHOOL 1892, HEADMASTER SINCE 1906

REV. F. E. LUCEY, IN KASHMIRI DRESS, BETWEEN THE HEADMASTER AND FIRST ASSISTANT

reported sick. By a coincidence, this festival had fallen on the first of April. The Principal thought it would be as well to visit the sick man, so he set off with a thermometer. When he reached the house he saw many shoes outside, which indicated that many guests were within. When he reached the sick man's room, however, all the guests had run away, and the master was lying on a bed of sickness. His temperature was normal, his pulse was normal, but the Principal looked serious and said he was sorry to hear of this sudden sickness; in fact, from the thermometer and the look of the master he was sending at once for medicine.

'Please, sir, do not trouble,' said the master.

'It is not a question of trouble, but of life and death. I should never forgive myself if you should die without medical aid.'

To cut a long story short, before noon on that April day, the master had to drink a good strong dose of aperient medicine, and next day he really had an excuse for staying at home.

Actually this master never came to our school again, for he ran away to another. He was later sent to Islamabad, a town thirty miles from Srinagar. There, for some years, he did all he could to smash our small branch school. He finally caught cholera and was dying. Our masters at Islamabad, hearing this, went to visit him, and found him deserted by all his companions. They stayed with him till the end, and finally heaped coals of fire upon him, literally as well as metaphorically, by carrying him to the cremation ground and paying all the expenses of his funeral.

Another master, during an epidemic, made himself quite ill by drinking too much cholera mixture. He was not ill himself at the time, but was trying to persuade others who had cholera to take the medicine. No one would take it till he did, for they thought he might be wishing to poison them.

Another time a master was dying of cholera at night. The Principal came to visit him, and found his brother masters massaging the body to relieve the terrible cramps. Next day the masters came to say that the patient was dead.

'What time did he die?' asked the Principal.

'When you gave him that spoonful of brandy.'

'But why did you not tell me then?'

'We did not want the people in the room to know; for they would have thought you had poisoned him; also women can stand bad news better in the daytime.'

Those wonderful men had continued all night massaging a corpse, knowing the risk they ran, in order to save the women a little of their sorrow.

The jobs that the staff have tackled are often very far off the track of ordinary schoolmastering, as the following story will show:

A very firm friend of the school had taken the contract for collecting the harvest of *singara* nuts from the Wular Lake. These nuts are the fruit of a water plant, and the State auctions the right of collecting them. They form the staple diet of the people living round the Wular.

The nuts are harvested by groups of boatmen who are responsible to certain headmen, and these, in turn, are responsible to the contractor appointed by the State.

On this occasion the contractor felt certain that the headmen were making false returns of the harvest. Being a European, and unacquainted with the intricacies of the business, he was at a loss to find out where the leakage was occurring. He needed some honest Kashmiris to go to the Wular and investigate for him. Thus it was that three of our staff were chosen to help him. These three men journeyed down separately to the Wular and stayed in the town of Sopor, which is the most important centre in that district. There, working independently and meeting secretly at night, they began to make discreet inquiries. Eventually they found out that on a certain night, in a village some miles away, a meeting was to be held of all the headmen concerned with the *singara* nut harvest. At the meeting they were going to decide what they should do with the surplus harvest that they had acquired. The main thing, however, was, that at the meeting a paper would be produced showing the true account of the harvest. On the night of the meeting one of the masters rode away to the village, while the other two waited on the Srinagar road with ponies ready. The rider neared the village, and in the distance he saw a large house with a light shining through a window. He dismounted outside the village, tied up his pony, and came in on foot. No one was about, for it was late, and country folk are early to rise and early to bed. He approached the house, took off his shoes, and stealthily made his way in. He crept down a passage, at the end of which a door stood ajar. He peeped in, and saw, seated on the floor, a group of men ranged round a brass stand on which were balanced a number of little dishes of oil, in each of which floated a flaming wick. The group of men were discussing a paper which was in the possession of one of them. Suddenly a form leapt into their midst, knocked over the brass lampstand, snatched the paper and was gone. They were sure the devil had visited them. Meanwhile outside, a man was hastily putting on his shoes, in a few seconds he was running through the deserted village, stuffing a paper in his pocket. He untied his pony, jumped on its back, and was off full gallop. Next morning three weary riders reached Srinagar, and the paper was delivered to its rightful owner.

One could go on with countless stories of kindness, unselfishness and bravery of these wonderful men, but space does not permit. Suffice it to say, that it would be hard to find more valiant men than there are among the staff.

Even so, the best of crews are liable at times to pick up scrimshankers, so that means have to be employed to eliminate passengers. For instance, any visitor to the school would notice that the staff all stand while teaching. In olden days it was a common sight to see the master asleep with his feet on a chair, while the boys fooled around him. Therefore, now no master, unless he be lame or over seventy, may sit down. There is one exception, however. The master whose room is considered the cleanest and tidiest, has a desk of honour at which he may sit, he also receives a bonus on his salary. If he be sensible and share his bonus with his pupils, the chair will remain with him, for the boys will be keen on keeping the room tidy.

Any account of the staff would be incomplete, without mention being made of some of those who, from time to time, have taken over the helm and given the steersman a spell.

Reference has already been made to the help rendered by the Rev. C. L'E. Burges and Mr. A. B. Tyndale. Shortly after their arrival, the Principal's brother, G. W. Tyndale-Biscoe, came out to Kashmir; besides taking over complete charge of the schools for a whole year, during the Principal's absence on leave, he also put in a great deal of foundation work; as, for instance, his system of monthly account sheets for each school, which system is in use at the present day.

For many years the Rev. F. E. Lucey worked in the schools as Vice-Principal, and did yeoman service in countless ways. Being an excellent mathematician, and a teacher who enjoyed teaching, he was able to keep the school up to the mark in the scholastic line; he was also a firm disciplinarian, which was a quality of inestimable value.

At Islamabad, Miss Coverdale, besides conducting her own girls' school, became Vice-Principal of the boys' school for many years, taking over all the administrative work connected with the accounts and character forms, etc. She also had the entire responsibility of the scripture teaching.

Our Honorary Treasurer, Mr. C. M. Hadow, has helped to steer us for many miles through the troubled waters of finance, both by his generosity and invaluable advice. His business insight in financial matters and his long experience of Kashmir, have many times and in many ways kept us clear of snags. His son, Major K. C. Hadow, is also always ready to take a turn at the tiller; especially has he been of help in giving instruction in boxing and athletics generally, and also in arousing the interest of others in our voyage.

Coming to more modern times, the name of the Rev. J. S. Dugdale will always be remembered with affection by the masters and boys who came in contact with him. He followed Mr. Lucey as Vice-Principal, and it would be hard to find a man who better followed his Master in the qualities of lovingkindness and humility. He gave us an example of our ideal, namely, the Christian gentleman.

Mr. R. Denton Thompson recently came to fill a gap for two years, during which time he interested the school in various branches of natural history. His energy in organising mountain trips was magnificent, seeing that he had lost a leg in the War. His agility on one leg should act as a spur to the Kashmiris to make better use of their two.

For many years Miss H. L'E. Burges has been connected with the school, and has given of her best. In years gone by she started the kindergarten department, and gave us the advantage of her Slojd training. She has also from time to time given the staff refresher courses in methods of teaching; and at the present time she is throwing herself into the task of making our technical branch a success.

It would take too long to continue this list of helpers, naming each one separately.[1] Nevertheless, they are all remembered with gratitude. Whatever they gave us of their knowledge or skill has added to our strength in pulling up stream and helped us to steer a straight course. May there be many more like them in the years to come.

---

[1] See Appendix on page 93.

300 BOYS LEAVE SCHOOL IN 25 SECONDS—A DAILY PRACTICE

BOYS JUMPING FROM THE SCHOOL ROOF INTO THE RIVER

CHAPTER XII

THE CHARACTER FORM

THIS chart is a combination of health certificate, mark register and terminal report. Each boy, on entering the school, is given a roll number and a page in the register, which is filled up twice a year.

The roll number helps us to find any boy in years to come after he leaves the school. His name tells us straight off what is his religion, from which at once we can get some idea of his character.

This story helps to show the difference between Hindus and Muhammadans.

A Hindu persuaded a Muhammadan to go shares with him in buying a cow. The Hindu then flattered the Muhammadan and said to him:

'As you are a great and noble man, I will give you first share in the cow, while I take the last share.'

The Muhammadan, being very pleased, agreed, so the Hindu said:

'Very well, then, you will have the front half of the cow while I have the hind-quarters.'

At feeding time the Hindu told the Muhammadan to look after his end, because the mouth was up there; but at milking time the Hindu said the hind-quarters were his business.

Coming back to the character form, we want to know about a boy's parents. His father's profession is a good indication of what to expect from the boy. While a merchant's son will be inclined towards honesty and and truth, there are other professions in which the reverse is the case. Again we are interested to know whether the boy has real parents or step-parents. Step-mothers here are often very hard on their step-children, so that, knowing this, we may be able to account for a boy's ill-health or timidity. Perhaps the step-mother is starving him so as to give better food to her own children.

Often a boy's 'father' changes; this may be due to his having been adopted by someone who has no son. This custom is very common with Hindus, who must have a son to pray for their souls in the next incarnation. A boy's 'father' may change for other reasons, as, for instance, a powerful

BOY'S CHARACTER FORM SHEET

Name............ *Son of*............ *Entered Central School*............ *Class*............ *193* . *Entered*............ *Branch School*

Roll No......... *Occpn. of* {*Guardian* / *Father*} .... *Left* „ „............ *Class*............ *193* . ...*193* . *Left*............ *193* .

Age *Years* *Months* *Days* *Date of Marriage* *Father's Salary* / *Probable Loot*

Date	Class	Age	Average Age of Class	Position in Class	Ears and Throat	Eyesight	Teeth	Height	Weight	Chest Measurement	General Health	Tutor
		Full Marks										

MIND									
English	Urdu or Hindi	Persian or Sanskrit	Science and Drawing	Mathematics	History } or { Physiology	Geography } or { Hygiene	Caligraphy	General Knowledge	Total
150	150	150	300	150	150	150	100	300	1,600

BODY						
Gymnastics	Boating	Swimming	Headers	Games: Cricket, Football, etc.	Manual Labour	Total
400	200	200	100	200	100	1,200

SOUL															
	CONDUCT TOWARDS						MANNERS				DISCIPLINE				
	Masters	Boys	School	City											
Scripture	Obedience, Respectfulness, Truthfulness, and Honesty	Pluck, Unselfishness and Good Temper	*Esprit de Corps*	Duty to Neighbours	Colour of Heart	Total	Deportment	Absence of Dirty Tricks	Self-control	Total	Cleanliness and Tidiness { Body / Clothes	Attendance	Punctuality	Total	
200	400	300	300	300		1,500	200	100	100	400	200	100	100	400	

Grand Total	Signature of Principal	Remarks
5,100		

man may have taken a fancy to the boy's mother and turned the father out of house and home. Priests seem to be the chief offenders in this line, because they have great powers.

We also wish to know whether a boy comes from a rich or poor home. The son of a rich man will naturally be better at games, for he gets better food and is therefore stronger. Also a fat boy, who can float, is better at swimming than a thin boy, who cannot. Again a rich boy can afford to send his clothes to the wash, so we are stricter about cleanliness with him than with a poor boy.

Notice also on the chart the date of marriage. When the school first started, nearly every boy was married, owing to the Hindu custom of early marriage. In order to check this bad custom, a fine was imposed on all boys marrying below eighteen years of age. This has reduced the married boys in the school to one per cent.

Before marking a boy we want to know about his health. We have a clinic attached to the school, with a qualified doctor in attendance. The boys are regularly inspected to see that no disease is starting. In this way we are able to check diseases at the beginning. Also in this clinic any minor ailments can be attended to, or boys advised to go to hospital for treatment. If any boy is reported sick, the compounder in charge of the clinic goes off to see if he is really sick or only shamming.

This health chart has been of great use where stupid masters are concerned. Often masters get angry with boys and accuse them of inattention, when the real trouble is deafness. Defective eyesight may be the cause of a boy's inability to read properly, and not negligence in preparing his lesson.

After the health chart the character form is divided into Mind, Body and Soul. Under mind come all his marks for class subjects, including general knowledge, which has been explained previously.

Under body he is marked not so much for proficiency at sport as for the keenness he shows. The reason for this was shown in the chapter on athletics.

Under soul the first thing is scripture. The Life of Christ is set before the boys as the highest example of manhood—the ideal after which we are striving. Each class hears the story of the Life of Christ every year, so a boy hears this whole story once for every year he is in the school. We teach this by maps, following our Lord's journeys in Palestine, noting the kind of country, time of year and the distances He travelled. Each place is noted for some kind act (just as in historical atlases, cross swords mark battlefields). We thus try to make the story a living account of things that happened during the noblest life that was ever lived.

Then under various heads come conduct towards masters, boys, school and city.

In the first section the form masters must, in consultation with others, use their own discretion.

In marking a boy for his duty towards the boys, his own class fellows do the work; they know best what a boy is worth for pluck and cheerfulness, etc. Also, if a master has favourites or the reverse, the class here have a chance of putting things right.

The section of duty to neighbours shows the marks which a master thinks a boy is worth for his willingness to do jobs for others. This is all explained in later chapters.

Marks for deportment largely depend upon the extent to which the boy has lost the 'pandit eye.'

In cleanliness we give a boy fifty marks straight off for a pocket handkerchief, as this saves the tail of his coat or the end of his *pugaree*. There is no need to enumerate and explain each section, for they are pretty clear. Suffice it to say, that unless each form master does his job thoroughly in visiting the boys and getting to know them, this character form would be meaningless.

Twice a year each boy stands before the Principal, and is asked if the marks are correct and fair. If he agrees the Principal puts his signature against them, and any remarks, as, for instance, the reason for a sudden rise or fall in marks, or any matter of interest that the master may have to report about the boy. If, however, the boy does not agree, and the master and the boy cannot come to agreement before the Principal, then the monitor of the class is called up. If these three cannot agree, then the class is asked to vote whether master or boy is right.

There then, when a boy leaves us, we have, as far as it is possible to know it, a true estimate of his worth as a citizen. If, in years to come, he returns to the school, seeking for a recommendation, there we can see what he agreed he was worth when he was with us.

Of course, this complicated chart has not grown in a day. It is the result of years of experience. New compartments have been added here

GUESTS AND PRIESTS AT THE MARRIAGE OF A BRAHMAN BOY

A HINDU CHILD MARRIAGE

and there, as the competence of the staff increased. The latest addition, and by far the hardest, is judging the colour of a boy's heart; we divide this into nearly thirty grades, from black to white.

As was said above, it is only when masters are doing their job properly that this chart can be of any value. It is soon possible to tell, by the way a master answers any of the questions put to him about his boys, whether he has really been taking any interest in them.

Perhaps this character form is the most important thing in the whole school. Through it we learn not only about the boys, but are able to know an enormous amount of what is going on in the great city of Srinagar. It is almost like a pulse, by which we can tell the health of far more than our school.

Being a day school, we have the boys under our direct care for a comparatively short time. If we are to make anything of them we must take responsibility for them during out-of-school hours as well. How can this be done unless we have some means of knowing how they live and occupy their spare time?

This character form gives us this information. It also lets the boys and parents know that we consider the boys are under our discipline in school and out, so long as their names are on our register.

Each boy receives a copy of his half-yearly character form, which he can take home and show to his parents.

Some parents are now actually beginning to take an interest in their boys' character forms. So we are getting along.

CHAPTER XIII

FIRES, THEOSOPHY, PESTILENCE AND FAMINE

THE reader who has travelled up stream with us so far will have noticed that mention is made in one or two places of social service. Now this is the most important subject that the boys learn in the school, and has done far more than anything else to turn their minds from selfishness to citizenship.

One of the first lessons they had in social service was at a big fire in the city. An English lesson was in progress one day, when a noise of shouting was heard from across the river, soon afterwards a bugle began to blare forth. The boys got up to see what was the cause of the trouble, and, having seen a thin column of smoke ascending, they realised it was only a fire, so they returned to their books.

What did it matter to them, none of their houses were affected? The young Englishman who was teaching them thought otherwise.

'Come along,' he said, 'let us go along and help at this fire.'

'No,' said the boys, 'we shall miss our lessons, and there is no need for us to go, for none of us live near there.'

However, whether they wished it or no, they did go, down the stairs, out of the school, through the streets, with the young Englishman bringing up the rear. When they reached the scene of the fire, what a sight it was! Women screaming and tearing out great bunches of hair, and rending their garments, in their efforts to get the onlookers to bring water. On the roof of a neighbouring house stood an arm of the law, blowing a bugle for all he was worth to attract his brothers, so that they might take any of the property they found into 'safe custody.'

A huge crowd of onlookers had assembled at the fire, but not a single soul would lift a finger to help put out the blaze until one of the women mentioned the word 'money.' Fierce bargaining ensued, and when the price had been forced up to about two annas per pot of water one or two of the more energetic began to bestir themselves.

The boys were soon arranged in a line from the house to the river, but they had no means of carrying water; a wise man, however, had brought up a large barge full of pots, and anchored out in midstream, waiting for the price to rise. Nothing would induce him to come nearer till one of the boys jumped into the river, boarded the barge, and brought it in by force. Then a steady line of water pots began to move towards the fire. The onlookers began to jeer at these Brahman coolies, and fellow Brahmans began to curse them. This was too much for the boys, so they compelled some of these haughty onlookers to take their place in the line.

That was the first fire at which our boys helped, albeit under compulsion. Since then they have helped at hundreds of fires. A small manual pump and fire buckets were installed in the school, and at every alarm people used to come running to the school, for it was the only fire brigade in a city built largely of wood, with one hundred and thirty thousand inhabitants.

Now, however, there is a municipal fire brigade, and the boys go not so much to fight the fire as to protect the property from would-be well-wishers, who wish to take care of it themselves.

In the town of Islamabad we have another school. There the citizens subscribed and bought a fire engine, at the suggestion of our headmaster. This they handed over to the care of our boys, so that in Islamabad our boys still form the only fire brigade. On one occasion they had to fight the flames for three days and nights.

It is interesting and illuminating to note that, in all the years in which our boys have helped at fires, only once has any owner of a house offered the boys a reward. Over and over again the boys have soiled and ruined their clothes in saving a rich man's house, and when the rich man has been asked if he would care to help the boys in renewing their clothes, he has always answered, 'Most certainly not.' On many occasions our boys and masters have been 'cut dead' or insulted on the very next day, by men whose houses and property they have been striving all night to save.

Gratitude is not the Kashmiri's strong suit.

Perhaps the most difficult piece of social work the school tackled in early days was sanitation. It very nearly smashed the school, for public opinion became so incensed.

Though the Brahman may befoul places, it is defilement for him to clean up his own mess. The only way to clean the place is to get a sweeper to do it, and this means parting with good hard cash. The consequence of this is that the public streets, and more especially the compounds of houses, and in winter, when it is too cold to go outside, even the houses themselves become unspeakably filthy. If it were not for those untiring, unpaid, uncared-for and despised municipal officers, the pariah dogs, Srinagar would long ago have become a buried city.

Now naturally the result of all this filth is that all sorts of diseases flourish and take a huge toll of life continually.

To give an example. Just outside the school was a cesspool. Over and over again the Principal had asked the municipality to have this pit filled in, but nothing was done.

Finally when three of the staff, one after the other, contracted typhoid and died, and their death was traced to this cesspit, the Principal spoke to the British Resident about it.

The British Resident came down to the school, and called the health officer of the district to meet him. This great gentleman was only too delighted to come; perhaps the British Resident was going to confer some honour on him?

The following conversation ensued:

British Resident: 'Are you the health officer in charge of this district?'

The great man (puffing up visibly): 'I am.'

British Resident: 'Are you in charge of this alley?'

The great man (protruding even further): 'I am.'

British Resident: 'Are you in charge of this spot?'

The great man (almost bursting with pride): 'I am.'

British Resident: 'You, filthy pig.'

When the great man had recovered from this pin which had so suddenly pricked his wind-bag, and was alone with the Principal, he said:

'Oh, sir, why did you not first ask me to fill in this hole before asking the British Resident down to the school?'

Nevertheless the hole was filled up.

That story gives an idea of what Srinagar used to be like when it was suggested that the school should form a sanitation corps. The plan was to get boys and masters to volunteer for this work, to persuade citizens to allow the corps to visit their homes, clean their compounds, and fill the cesspits with sand from the river-bed.

All seemed to be going well, but under the surface the forces of religion had started to work. Secretly men visited the parents of boys, and

THE SCHOOL FLEET OUTSIDE THE BOATHOUSE ON THE DAL LAKE

ROLL CALL IN THE DAL LAKE

terrorised them by threatening them with terrible consequences if their boys should engage in this degrading work.

A day had been fixed for the corps to start its work, by visiting the mission ladies' dispensary, which neighbours were using as a dumping ground for their refuse. The Principal came down to school in a boat, in which were shovels and picks. As soon as he entered the school he saw something was wrong. He called for volunteers. One Muhammadan came and stood at his right hand. With a little hesitation a Brahman came and stood at his left side. Then, as if with a concerted move, the whole school, masters and boys, covering their faces with blankets, rose up and bolted. In a few minutes, the Principal and his two faithful attendants stood alone in an empty school. The secret workers had done their job thoroughly.

'Never mind,' said the Principal, 'we three will go and make a start.'

They got into the boat, and set off for their destination. On a bridge near by was a crowd of howling citizens; the three men in the boat, therefore, stood up and gave their audience three cheers before proceeding. When they arrived, they found that quite a crowd of boys and masters had also foregathered, having come secretly by devious routes, not daring to face the public journey by water.

For the rest of that day this first brave band set to work with a will. Soon a huge crowd assembled outside to jeer and threaten. The boys had burned their boats however, and began to take a delight in pitching the muck out of the compound on to the mob outside.

The whole city had now began to hum. A public meeting was called in the school, when Dr. Arthur Neve tried to show the people that this work was to save their lives. But no, it was against their religion, and fanaticism won the day.

To show the strength of popular prejudice against sanitation, the following anecdote will serve. On a later occasion, when the authorities were trying to pave a filthy alley, priests came and lay down in the muck to hinder operations.

It was during this fight for a clean city that the school came to know for certain who were its friends and who its enemies. There was a fine old magistrate of the city at that time, whose son was in the school. He ordered that his son was to carry a shovel on his shoulder whenever he rode on his gaily caparisoned horse to and from school, in order to show the city that the governor was in favour of sanitation.

It was now that Mrs. Annie Besant became perturbed, on hearing the terrible news of a missionary who was deliberately breaking the caste of the Brahman. Among other yarns she heard, and had published in forty different Indian papers, was this one: 'Mr. Biscoe makes his Brahman boys drag dead dogs through the streets of Srinagar.'

Again Taffy, the faithful spaniel, became of service. One of his accomplishments was dying for Queen Victoria; he was accordingly ordered to die, not for Queen Victoria this time, but for Annie Besant instead. A rope was tied to him, and boys posed for a photograph, holding the rope. A photograph was taken to show that anyhow one of Mrs. Besant's yarns was true.

Before coming up to Kashmir, Mrs. Besant had got into communication with a member of the staff, who played the part of Judas to perfection. The staff mutinied, and three hundred boys left in a fortnight to join Mrs. Besant's Theosophical school, in a large building just opposite their old school.

Mrs. Besant ingratiated herself with the authorities, and money was showered upon her to make her school a success. Agents were sent round to warn parents that their boys would not get State employ if they remained in the Mission school.

Finally, at the crest of her wave, there were left in our school only some half dozen boys and the loyal masters who had not joined the mutiny.

Gradually Mrs. Besant's meteoric popularity waned. Perhaps also she had learnt something of the Kashmiri Brahman at first hand, of which she had never dreamed in her remote Theosophical paradises in South India.

Anyhow, Mrs. Besant went away, let us hope a wiser woman. Her school was taken over by the State. Our numbers began to go up, till within a year they were more than they had been before the fight. Many of the old boys tried to return, but the conditions imposed for re-admission were so severe that few of them dared to face the music.

This fight took place in the year 1901, and it was a whole year before the school was finally steered safely into smoother waters. How nearly this fight cost the Principal his life, only he and the doctors who afterwards attended him can say.

Just to show how completely the fight for sanitation has been won, there is only need to bring things up to date. In the year 1929 the municipality decided to give His Highness the Maharaja the novel birthday present of a clean city. Our school was asked to co-operate, and for a whole fortnight, by propaganda, processions and posters, the citizens were urged to clean their houses and compounds. The boys also were allotted areas for the cleanliness of which they made themselves responsible. Every day, before and after school, they worked with the help of the authorities, till the city looked as it had never looked before. Mrs. Besant was not consulted on this occasion.

Mention was made earlier in this chapter of the diseases which cause such terrible havoc. Of all these, perhaps the most dreaded was cholera, though in these days, of a municipal water supply and inoculation, its terrors have been considerably lessened. It is always a matter of wonder that, though the citizens at first resolutely boycotted the water supply, they have taken to inoculation with eagerness.

In the early days, the only water for all purposes was from the river and canals. As the filth of the city gradually oozed into these waterways, it is not surprising that cholera was a very terrible scourge.

About every third year, at the beginning of the summer, cholera used to appear at the head of the valley, introduced by infected Hindu pilgrims entering Kashmir; from that quarter it would then make its way down stream till it reached the city. Then it would rage furiously, till with the approach of winter it gradually petered out and disappeared.

The city, during the height of an epidemic, would become like a city of the dead. Utterly resigned to their fate, the inhabitants would shut themselves into their houses, and thus try to keep the disease out. All shops would close; in fact, the appearance of Srinagar probably resembled that of London during the Great Plague.

The first attempts at fighting cholera which the school made were directed towards cheering up the inhabitants, and inducing them to come out into the fresh air.

The schools were, of course, kept open, and organised games were continued with renewed vigour. The whole fleet of boats would paddle up and down the river, singing, shouting and making a loud noise, so that the citizens would come out to see the *tamasha*. Our boys died like others, but their places in the boats were filled each day by others. Seeing that boys were thus induced to become more cheerful, and apparently did not decrease in numbers, the citizens became more cheerful, and one of the predisposing causes of disease was thus removed.

More active steps than this, however, were needed if lives were to be saved. In every school was a large supply of cholera mixture, and a man with a bicycle was always on duty, day and night, to ride off with medicine, whenever anyone should bring news of a patient.

In an earlier chapter an example was given of the difficulty our men encountered in persuading patients to take medicine.

In one epidemic they were able to save over two hundred lives from cholera by the prompt delivery of medicine.

Since the introduction of tap water cholera has become much less, and the people of the city do not hide in their houses. Our schools are still useful, however, in helping the medical authorities with their fight, for we are only too glad that they should use our schools as centres where the general public, as well as our boys, may receive inoculation.

We now come to the last section of this chapter—Famine. It is not often that a school has been able to be of service in stopping a famine, and, fortunately, only once has the school had to do this work.

To understand this famine, which started in 1918 and dragged on for about three years, we must go back about fifty years. In the year 1877–79, owing to irregularities in the land revenue department, the peasants were not allowed to reap their harvest, and the result was one of the worst famines in the history of Kashmir. The people of the city, however, did not suffer, for the Government gave them free rice from the huge granaries that had been filled with the tribute of the peasants during previous years.

As a result of this, Mr. Lawrence (now Sir Walter Lawrence) was lent by the Government of India to the Kashmir State to survey the whole valley, and have the revenue put on to a permanent and satisfactory basis.

During his work up here Sir Walter Lawrence foretold a swing of the pendulum, when the villagers would have abundance and would starve the city folk.

Here a digression is permissible, as it is such an excellent example of the Kashmiri's cheerfulness under depressing circumstances. Sir Walter Lawrence tells how, during the time when he was touring the villages on his great work of bringing prosperity to their inhabitants, for which to this day his name is remembered with gratitude in the remotest corners of the valley, he happened to be approaching a village when he saw a most extraordinary sight. It seemed as if a man were standing on his head, waving his legs in the air; in fact, on closer inspection, that was what it was.

SOCIAL SERVICE

MASTERS SUPERVISING THE DISTRIBUTION OF RICE DURING FAMINE
(See page 60)

RUINS OF ISLAMABAD AFTER THE FIRE, WHICH THE SCHOOL FOUGHT FOR THREE DAYS AND NIGHTS (See page 54)

A GROUP OF FIRE FIGHTERS

'What are you doing in that extraordinary position?' said Mr. Lawrence.

'Oh, *Sahib*,' answered the ruined villager, 'my affairs are in such a muddle that I don't know whether I am standing on my head or my heels.'

In 1918, owing to a poor harvest, the price of rice went up; the following year was a bumper harvest, but the rice merchants (called *galadars*) arranged with the villagers to hold back the rice, and so force up prices even higher. Sir Walter Lawrence's prophecy was coming true. This policy was continued during the third year. Not only did the rice merchants carry out this practice, but the butchers, firewood merchants, and, in fact, all the suppliers of vital necessities followed suit by cornering the whole year's supply.

To give some idea of the price of commodities, rice rose to eight times its normal price, and rice is the staple diet of the Kashmiris; in fact, one might say that ninety-five per cent. of a Kashmiri's food is rice. For the poor folk in the city this, of course, meant starvation.

For various reasons the State was powerless to put a stop to this terrible state of affairs. During the height of this scandal a strong governor was appointed to the city. He really wished to put things right, but had no one on whom he could rely to carry out his instructions. It was then that the school and staff put themselves at his disposal.

The schools were closed. The staff were sent off to scour the valley for hidden rice barges, and compel the boatmen to bring them in.

As soon as the boats began to come in the frenzied citizens fell upon them, and tore and trampled each other to get at the grain. It was, therefore, necessary to tie the boats in midstream and to bring one or two purchasers at a time in small boats.

The question now was, who should be served first? Our men decided to serve the women first. Next day no men came, but all sent their women folk for them. So the staff then gave preference to women carrying babies. Next day every woman had a baby. So the staff had to choose women with two children.

A system of ration tickets was instituted, so that no one could buy more than his needs. On one occasion the crowd at one of these rice depôts was astonished to see one of our masters hold up a good silver rupee, and pitch it into the river with the remark, 'See this man? He offers me a rupee if I will give him a double ration.'

Meanwhile the governor was taking a firm line with the profiteers. One of his punishments was to shave off half the beards of those he caught, and, placing them on donkeys, facing the tail, to parade them round the city.

The experiences of our staff were many and varied. Often they were cheered and blessed as they walked through the streets, while at other times, when they passed provision stores, curses would be rained upon them.

This is one of the remarks heard as a party of our men were walking through the streets: 'There go the hounds of hell, let loose upon this city by Padre Biscoe.'

Towards the end of this fight, when things had practically become normal, the strong governor died, to the great loss of Kashmir. Finally, through the intervention of the Viceroy, Lord Reading, the State took over the whole of the rice supply, buying it from the villagers and selling it from central granaries at a fair price to the people of the city. This system is still in force?

At another time, though not during this famine, one of our men saw a boat, full of rice, tethered in mid-stream, while some poor women were beseeching the boatman to come to shore and sell to them. Our master quickly went home, where he had a fine, long, blue coat with brass buttons, which he had inherited from his father, who had been a State official. Putting on this coat and a smart, high *pugaree*, and carrying a silver-knobbed stick, he returned to the river. Putting his stomach well out, he shouted to the boatman, 'Bring that boat in here.' The boatman, thinking he was some high official, hastened to obey. As soon as the boat had come in, the 'brass hat' ordered the boatman to sell rice to the women, and stayed beside him till the women had been satisfied. This man is now a magistrate, where he can and does deal out justice to punish the wrong-doers and help the oppressed. The four headings of this chapter give some idea of the general way in which our boys, while they are still at school, learn, through the example of their masters, to serve their country.

A citizenship book is kept, in which are recorded all the various deeds of social service which are reported by the citizens to the staff. The boys are firmly discouraged from reporting on their own prowess.

This book shows how, in a hundred and one ways, the boys, either in groups or individually, are learning to keep their eyes open and to use their gifts for others.

In winter, the boys help old or weak neighbours, by clearing the snow off their roofs, to prevent the houses collapsing. They carry numerous loads for the weak and aged. They find lost children and blind people, and guide them home. They find owners of lost property. In fact, wherever there is a job to be done, the boys learn to be willing to do it, regardless of religious or caste inhibitions.

Thus it is we hope, that now their eyes have come off the loot, they will look on State service, or any profession they may take up, not so much with an eye to what they will get as to what they will give.

CHAPTER XIV

BEGGARS AND BANKERS

OF all things the Kashmiri hates doing, perhaps parting with money hurts him most. It is amazing, the difficulty we still have in getting parents to pay fees. Even rich men will try to evade paying sixpence a month for their sons' education. The highest fees we can charge in the top class are about two shillings a month, while the lowest are about two pence. This is because we have to compete with free schools, ours being the only school which charges any fees.

If the Kashmiri objects to paying for his cake, how much more does he hate paying for no cake. It is almost impossible to get a Kashmiri to subscribe to any charity or to help any deserving person who is in distress.

By a curious twist of the mind though, one will often see passers-by throwing coins to the beggars who swarm in the streets of Srinagar. Though they know quite well the beggar is a fraud, still they give him their pice, for it piles up merit for them in the next world.

These beggars are of both sexes. Many of them are quite strong and healthy, but they find it more profitable to beg than to work. At one time the staff investigated the condition of every beggar in Srinagar, and traced them to their homes. The school offered employment and regular wages to any of them who were really infirm.

Only one crippled beggar accepted the offer, and, as he could only crawl on hands and knees, he was made the school porter, and his work was to stay by the entrance to prevent people passing in or out unlawfully. He was specially useful for this job, because he possessed a sepulchral voice and could bark like a dog; he could thus be porter or watchdog, as occasion demanded. He was also provided with needle and thread, and was able to earn a few pence by sewing on boys' buttons and doing odd jobs of mending. Three times he tired of this prosaic way of earning a living, and ran away. Three times he was brought back, and the last time he stayed till the day of his death.

All the well-known beggars, who sit along the roadside of the European quarter in the summer and on Sundays, to soften the hearts of Europeans,

A GROUP OF MODERN ATHLETES

TWO GLIMPSES OF THE SCHOOL COMPOUND DURING THE DAILY DRILL PERIOD

THE SCHOOL BAND

are frauds. One famous woman, who sits with a baby and moans piteously when any European passes, went to one of our old boys, who is a shopkeeper, to change her earnings into notes. She had collected five pounds and over. We had her traced, and found that she has a husband, who sits at home idle while she begs for him. She hires a baby for the day from a neighbour, and pinches it to make it cry when a wealthy-looking European passes.

Others, who are 'cripples,' can be seen running and singing in the city when their day's 'work' is over. We found that there is a prince of beggars, who runs the lot and arranges their beats, so that there shall be no overlapping or quarrelling. For these services he takes a percentage of their earnings.

It is a sad thing to note the increasing tendency of the Kashmiris to go in for begging, with the advent of Europeans in greater numbers, now that motors have made Kashmir more accessible. The whole trouble often starts because kind-hearted visitors will tip children who come up and say, '*Sahib*, *salaam*, *bakshish*.'

It is becoming increasingly common for children now to go in for this begging, and, if they find there is easy money to be made in this way, naturally many of them make it their life's profession.

But to return to the Kashmiri who gives to beggars. He, unlike the European, knows they are frauds. It was in order to encourage any little springs of charity that the boys might possess, that in each classroom was placed a poor box, as mentioned in a previous chapter. The idea was to divert these springs into the right channels, instead of into the pockets of beggars. In the first year that this organised charity was started, the whole school of three hundred boys in one year subscribed about three shillings. Now each class collects annually from one to three pounds.

The money so collected is now either used to support a poor boy in the class, or to help poor people in real distress whom the boys or masters come across. Of this class, perhaps the most miserable are the Hindu widows; in a later chapter, however, will be found a description of how the school has tried to champion them. The boys also collect money to provide refreshments for the hospital patients whom they take for joy-rides in the school boats.

Besides this organised charity, the school engaged in another activity to do with money.

In the early years every master was deeply in debt. Most of these debts were inherited from their fathers, who had borrowed large sums from the State, probably to pay for weddings. Over and over again, a young master, just starting in life, would suddenly receive a bombshell in the shape of a huge bill, for thousands of rupees to be paid within a certain date, failing which he would be sold up lock, stock and barrel.

Others were in the hands of blood-suckers, who charged anything up to 150 per cent. interest per annum. To remove this curse, and free the staff, a fund was started. Masters were asked to subscribe to the fund and receive 5 per cent. on their deposits, while the fund advanced money at 10 per cent. The whole of this fund actually belongs to the staff. It is a sort of co-operative bank.

By means of this loan fund all the staff have been freed from debt. The fund, of course, increased, and we were able to extend its offer to the general public. Later on, owing to the amount of work this entailed for the staff, we had to limit our sphere to old boys of the school.

Money is advanced to help anyone out of debt, to buy, build or repair his house, or to start a man in business. We will not on any account lend money to be squandered on a marriage. It is etiquette to get deeply in debt for marriages, and we do not wish to encourage this wasteful custom.

Every applicant has to furnish good security, in the person of someone of property, who will refund the debt in case the applicant fails us.

Every application is first investigated by a member of the staff, to see that the security is sound and also to see that the money is really needed for the purpose stated. The investigating master has to go to the very spot to see the house which needs repair, or whatever it is.

To show how important these investigations are, the following account is given:

A man applied for a loan to start a business. The loan was granted on condition of the usual security, and after a master should have investigated the matter, to make sure the man was not going to use the money for some other purpose, such as a wedding. The investigating master finally reported that it was quite true that the loan was wanted for business, the business being traffic in women. The loan was not granted.

This loan fund, of course, could never function without the untiring efforts of our masters, and it says a lot for their efficiency, when one realises that only about twice have they failed to make defaulters pay up.

Many times they have had to take cases to court, entailing endless hours of trouble, but the fund has succeeded.

Not only has the fund increased in wealth, making a tidy little sum for the staff on retirement, but countless homes have been relieved of the nightmare of debt. Many families are living in comfortable houses, and numbers of old boys have been able to set up on their own in business.

CHAPTER XV

ANIMALS

IN their attitude towards animals, perhaps more than anything else, does religion play queer tricks with the Kashmiri mind.

First of all, both Hindus and Muhammadans are against taking life, though both communities are very partial to flesh and fowl,[1] and the Kashmiri equivalent of the good red herring.

A Hindu must not take life because he believes in re-incarnation. Many a time a boy, after searching diligently in his clothing for the cause of the trouble, will at last find his quarry; instead of despatching it summarily, he becomes filled with compassion for his one-time irritant; so, when his next door neighbour is not looking, he puts his little friend out to graze on pastures new.

In the early days, whenever an impious Englishman tried to rid himself of a persistent fly, the whole class would draw in their breath or suck their fingers with horror. The blunt question from the fly murderer, 'Do you eat mutton?' was unanswerable.

It is doubtful whether to this day one could find many Brahman boys who would deliberately kill a noxious insect.

The Muhammadans are also averse to taking life, or even pruning trees or pulling up weeds; for, unless it be a question of food or clothing, they consider that the Creator put these things there; and who is man to interfere with the Divine plan? Because of this idea, the method of 'killing' rats, which are a veritable plague, is to take them, when caught in traps, to the other side of the river, and then release them. As people live on both banks of the river, and both sides go in for this game, it is pretty obviously stalemate.

Besides this aversion to killing, of course the cow is holy to the Hindus and in Kashmir the death penalty was inflicted about sixty years ago for cow-killing. Now the penalty is seven years' imprisonment. The consequence is that there are far too many cows, and numbers have to die miserable

[1] The Hindu may eat all kinds of wild fowl and their eggs, but may not eat tame fowl or their eggs. This also applies to ducks and geese.

deaths from disease, starvation, and old age. Also the Muhammadans, who form the bulk of the population, do not consider the cow holy, and have, therefore, no scruples about causing a cow to die a slow 'natural' death, to prevent its eating up the grass which they want for their better cattle.

The pious regard of the Hindu for cows has no concern with their suffering. Often in the winter a wretched cow will fall down from weakness. A Brahman walking by will see the dogs, crows and kites collecting round, waiting to start as soon as the cow is too weak to move. He will piously touch the cow with his sleeve, and place the sleeve to his lips, and with an inward glow of satisfaction he will proceed. A short time later he will pass that way again, and pass the remains of what was once a cow before the snarling dogs had got at it to tear it to pieces while still alive. He will now shudder, and draw his clothes around him, lest he should touch the remains, for a corpse is defilement. His reverence for the cow does not get to the stage of seeing that at least it shall die in peace.

Just as the cow is holy, so are many animals unclean, notably dogs, and to Hindus, donkeys. Though dogs are utterly unclean to both communities, yet no one thinks of killing a mad dog. In fact, one of our Brahman masters, who was the first man to take up this work (and brave work it is, too, to tackle a mad dog and kill it with only a stick, for the Kashmiri dogs are large), was boycotted by his neighbours. For a long time they would not sell him food or have any dealings with him. He had rid their neighbourhood of many mad dogs, and saved them from a dreadful scourge. Yet, because he was a Brahman, he had done the unforgivable thing, the taking of life.

One may drive a pony till it drops with fatigue and dies from exhaustion. One may drive over a dog and break its legs, but to put either of these quickly out of their misery is sin.

It can be seen then that, in tackling the question of prevention of cruelty to animals, a good many prejudices had to be overcome.

The first attempts in this direction were the obvious ones of finding starving animals and feeding them. This was more in accordance with the popular idea on the subject, and consequently fairly easy of attainment. One winter the boys found in the streets over a hundred starving donkeys and brought them to the school. There they were fed and cared for till the spring, when the owners came to reclaim them. They were handed over when the owners had paid the cost of their keep.

Boys then began to sit beside dying cows, to prevent the birds pecking them or dogs tearing them before they were dead.

The next stage was that they began to notice limping pack ponies and donkeys; later they were able to discover those that had galled backs under their loads, by the peculiar way they have of swinging their heads. They would then persuade the owner to free his animal, the persuasion being either gentle or forcible, according to the nature of the owner. On many occasions little boys, being unable to make the owners free their animals, have shared the load with the animal themselves. This is very wonderful, when one realises that a Brahman is helping an unclean donkey.

The following story is not so remarkable on account of the cruelty of the individual, for there are cruel individuals in all parts of the world; but shows the attitude of the public towards cruelty:

An Englishman some years ago noticed a man coming along very slowly, seated on a pony. The man seemed quite contented with his slow progress, for he was singing gaily to himself. On coming near the Englishman noticed that the pony was limping badly, so he went towards it to investigate the trouble.

The cause of the limp was that one of the pony's forelegs was broken in two places, with the bone protruding through the skin.

Now the man had been riding on that pony along the high road for quite a distance. There were many people using that road, yet not a single soul had thought that there was anything remarkable in the sight.

However, there are some Kashmiris who have got a new pair of eyes with regard to this sort of cruelty, as the following story shows:

One day the school was surprised to see a pair of donkey's ears appearing over the wall. No one could make out what they were doing so high up, until a few moments later a donkey came into school riding on its owner's back, with our headmaster bringing up the rear.

The headmaster had seen the man riding this donkey dead lame, so he had caused the tables to be turned, and brought the man to school as an object lesson to the boys.

Once it was started, however, the idea of kindness to animals soon spread. We find many cases where Muhammadan boys have taken the bones out of dogs' throats. This needs considerable pluck, when one remembers that these dogs are practically wild and in pain. The boys

A DONKEY SAVED FROM STARVATION DURING THE WINTER

A PONY RESCUED FROM BEING DRIVEN ALONG THE ROAD IN THIS CONDITION

CREWS WHO TOOK OUT THE GREATEST NUMBER OF SICK PATIENTS FOR JOY RIDES IN THEIR BOATS DURING ONE YEAR

have often had to borrow tongs from blacksmiths to reach the bone, and the blacksmith, being a Muhammadan, usually needs a good deal of 'persuasion.'

Blood is also a defilement to the Brahman. Yet, one small Hindu boy covered himself with blood in saving a puppy from drowning in a slaughter-house drain.

Boys have, on occasions, run great risk in saving animals from burning houses and from drowning. One could go on indefinitely with the countless acts of kindness to donkeys, horses, cows, dogs, cats and even birds that the boys accomplish every year, but space does not permit. Enough has been said to indicate that the outlook has changed, and the poor animals of Kashmir have at last got some true champions.

CHAPTER XVI

KNIGHTS ERRANT

ONE has only to contemplate the condition of women in Kashmir to realise what a long way the country has still to travel before it can take its place among the other nations of the world. Shut away in *purdah*, with a thousand and one rules preventing them from enjoying the simple pleasures of fresh air and sunlight, a large section of the women are not, to all intents and purposes, part of the population at all.

Being weaker than men, they have been driven to the wall. It is still a common sight to see women literally going to the wall to make way for men, by treading into the deep snow so that the lords of creation may pass. The women know full well that if they do not make way they will be pushed roughly to one side.

It used to be a great sight in the early days of the school to see a great gentleman making his way to office at about 12.30 p.m. Offices open at 10 a.m., but the greater the man the later he arrives. With stomach well out, and umbrella spread, the great man proceeded at the stately pace of two miles per hour. Behind him came his juniors, in due order of seniority, one carrying books, another papers and office files for the great one, and so on, in number anything up to thirty or so, forming a regular comet's tail.

Every now and then the great one would fling some sentence over his shoulder to his satellites, who, bending low at the honour, would send back the answer which they thought he would like best.

Slowly the stately column advanced through the narrow track in the snow.

A man bearing a load would approach from the other direction, and would step aside into the deep snow to let the great one pass. A woman, with a water-pot, would have to stumble bare-legged into the knee-deep snow, while the well-covered gentleman passed on his way. Similarly, children must make room for the great one.

Cows and dogs, on the other hand, are no respecters of persons. The thought of a horn in the stomach or a nip in the fleshy part of the calf of his leg makes the great one step nimbly aside, so that brute creation may pass.

It was the continual sight of processions such as this that sowed the seed from which sprouted the social service system of the school. The beginnings of this system were made by the formation of a Knights Errant Society, whose members promised to be chivalrous towards women.

Every day the Principal walked down to school with a party of young masters, and whenever they met a woman they stepped aside to let her pass. It was a difficult job, for the ladies could not understand what these men were doing, and instinctively mistrusted them (good cause, too, they had for mistrusting men), often it was quite a long time before the ladies would pass on; but it was a rule of the society that they would not proceed until the ladies had passed.

Another common sight in those days were the struggles of the women in carrying the heavy water-pots.

Here is an actual example. It was a cold winter's day, and a crowd of men were sitting over their fire-pots, smoking hookahs and taking snuff by the water's edge. A woman, carrying a baby, came down with her large two-gallon pot for water. The muddy banks were slippery with slush and snow. The woman filled the pot, with a heave she got it unto her knee, another heave and she had it on her shoulder, and then one more heave and it was balanced on the top of her head.

She started slowly to make her way up the slippery bank. One arm encircled the baby under her *pheran*, under which she also carried her fire-pot, her free hand she used for steadying the water-pot. Suddenly she slipped, down went the water-pot with a crash. The fire-pot upset inside the woman's *pheran*, scattering live charcoal all over her and the child. The child, of course, started to scream, the woman was helpless, as her arms were entangled in her *pheran*. Not one of the smokers or snuff-takers ceased smoking or taking snuff. One glance, to see what all the screaming was about, was all the notice they took of the incident.

It was not long before the Knights Errant had learnt to carry loads for women, though it is only within recent years that boys have become brave enough to be seen carrying water-pots. They would carry bags of rice, loads of firewood, or even babies, but not water-pots. Water-pot carrying is *par excellence* women's work, and it is very degrading for a man to do such a thing; in much the same way as an English boy would be ashamed to be seen doing the darning or mending.

While talking of load-carrying, here is an amusing story. One of the staff saw a woman carrying a baby and a bundle. He went up and offered to carry the load for her, but she refused. So he said, 'Look here, here are two rupees. Take them, and when you get your load back safely from me you can return the money.' Hearing this, the woman accepted his services and handed him the baby instead.

His two rupees were duly returned when he delivered the baby safe and sound at the woman's house.

We must once again look back to the early days, before following the progress of the Knights Errant to the present day.

A class was in progress, when outside in the street someone began to scream. The Principal went to the window, and there he saw a young man kicking a woman on the shin with his heavy wooden clog.

'Come here,' said the Principal to the boys. When they, too, had reached the window, he pointed to the scene below and said, 'Do you think that is a pretty sight?'

'Oh, he is only kicking his mother,' they said. Within a very short time, staff and boys had been ordered out into the street.

'Seize that man,' the Principal said to a lusty young master, 'and make him apologise to his mother.' The young man refused to apologise.

'Into the river with him then.'

The young master clasped the youth round the middle and jumped with him into the river.

'Now, will you apologise?'

'No,' said the youth.

'Duck him then.'

After a few moments the head was allowed up, and again he was asked to apologise to his mother. Again he refused. Again he went down. At last after several duckings he came out weeping, and had to put his head between his mother's feet and apologise in the true Eastern fashion.

Needless to say, his mother had been clutching the Principal firmly by the ankles and imploring forgiveness for her son from the very moment he had been seized. Since then all young men who wished to kick their mothers have taken care to do it out of sight and hearing of our school.

One of the great difficulties of would-be Knights Errant were the horrible insinuations against their good name which they had to bear. No one could understand any man speaking to a woman, let alone helping her, except for one purpose. The women, too, were naturally suspicious.

However, those days, thank God, are gone, and the women even trust our boys to take them out from the hospitals for joy rides in their boats. Over one thousand women were entertained in this way in one year. Our boys no longer feel shy of speaking to women. This is partly due to the number of English ladies who have come to the school to help to teach the boys, and have also allowed the boys to help them in various ways. It has, so to speak, softened the bump. The boys did not feel quite so queer in speaking to their own country-women after having first learnt how to behave towards English ladies.

It was through one of these ladies that the next step in the drama took place. Dr. Kate Knowles came out to work among the women, and she it was who found out all about the terrible sufferings of the women in their homes. Sufferings which the men had hidden from prying European eyes by means of the sanctity of their zenanas.

It would take far too long to describe all the terrible tortures and cruelties which are inflicted on the women of this land, and especially Hindu women, in the name of religion. If the reader should wish to know of this, most of it is written in Katherine Mayo's book, *Mother India.*

All the dreary, ghastly consequences of child-marriage,[1] unequal marriage, where immature girls are married to old and diseased men, enforced widowhood, the terrible child-birth customs, whereby children must be born on certain days, even though it means using artificial methods to accelerate or retard delivery. All these became known, and that was half the battle.

It is possible to fight a known enemy, and the Knights Errant were shown that they had got to do something far harder than merely carrying water-pots.

The traffic in women was also another enemy for the Knights to tilt at, though this was at least an open enemy.

Girls are often kidnapped and carried off, to become the stock-in-trade of those devils who go in for the business.

On one occasion the parents of a girl came to us to help them in saving their little girl, who had been kidnapped in this way. With the aid of the police the house was raided, and the little girl returned to her parents. During the trial that resulted from this, the proprietress of the

[1] In 1928 H.H. the Maharajah passed a law forbidding the marriage of any girl within his dominions under fourteen years of age.

establishment said that our masters had got up the whole thing to spite her, because she would not have anything to do with them.

Similar to this work was the suppression of a gang which was indulging the pastime of molesting unprotected women. This story, too, is an example of humour winning the battle, coupled with ability for acting, which is very common among the Kashmiris.

It was noticed that one of the staff was looking distinctly wretched, but denied that he was ill. Eventually enquiries by his brother-masters showed that he was very worried because his wife was being bullied by a regular organised gang. This gang was led by a priest, who had so much power that no men were able to defend their women from him, or take action against him.

In Kashmir the women have to go to the river to wash either in the early dawn or after dusk, so as to avoid the men. This gang, therefore, knowing that their husbands would not be about to protect their ladies, chose these times to carry on this work. They used to seize these defenceless women, and beat them till they had extracted certain promises from them; and then, under cover of darkness, they used to escape.

The influential priest, leader of this gang, was invited to come to the school. On his arrival he was accorded a cordial welcome by the Principal, staff and boys.

He was then invited to address the assembled school, which, after hesitating a little, he was pleased to do.

'Boys,' said the Principal in introducing him, 'we have here a very great and famous man. It is seldom that we have had the honour of being addressed by a priest of such high standing. Let us give three cheers for our great visitor.'

The school responded with three resounding cheers, and the visitor was evidently delighted with his reception.

After he had spoken a few words to the boys, the Principal thanked him and again turned to the school:

'Boys,' he said, 'we have all been greatly honoured by the words our visitor has so kindly delivered, but, being a modest man, he has not mentioned anything of his great prowess as a fighter and of his great bravery; we all like to honour brave men, so let us give three cheers to the visitor for his great bravery.'

Again the school rang with three lusty cheers, and the Principal continued:

'We all here know something about boxing and fighting; but we have not attained the distinction for which this gentleman is justly famous. We have not gone in for fighting and beating women.'

Here the visitor began to say he ought to be going, but the Principal urged him to stay. At this point a commotion was heard outside in the playground.

'Who is making all that commotion outside?' asked the Principal.

A master went out, and reported that a woman had come in and was weeping.

'Why, that is the very thing we want; here, bring her in at once. This gentleman will be able to give us a practical demonstration of his strength and bravery.'

Again the visitor made an attempt to leave, but was detained.

In a few minutes the woman was dragged into the school hall, doubled up with grief and choking with sobs. What did it matter that she bore a strong resemblance to one of the boys, whose place at the moment was, by a coincidence, empty? How should the visitor know that?

'Bring a cane,' was the next order, 'and give it to this gentleman, so that he may here and now show us all exactly how he does it.'

Above the wails of the woman the visitor was at last able to make himself heard.

'Sir,' he said, 'I think you are making fool of me.'

'Boys,' said the Principal, 'this gentleman thinks we are fooling him, and in this he proves that not only is he a great man and a brave man, but also a wise man. Let us, therefore, for the third time, unite in giving him three cheers, on account of his remarkable wisdom.'

For the third time the school rang out with three lusty cheers. The staff and Principal shook their visitor heartily by the hand, and, again thanking him for his kindness in visiting the school, bade him farewell. That was the last that was heard of that gang.

This next story tells of a Kashmiri Sir Lancelot. It took place in 1927, which shows that there is still plenty for Knights Errant to do.

One afternoon, one of our Brahman boys was paddling his uncle along in a boat. Suddenly he heard cries from another boat; on getting close, he found that three girls had paid a boatman to take them home; the boatman, having got them at his mercy, was taking them off for his own purposes.

The boy immediately paddled hard and caught up with the enemy, and, while his uncle helped the girls into their boat, he boarded the enemy and seized the paddle from the boatman and started to thrash him. The boatman's female relations then came to rescue him, so our boy had to return. He kept the paddle, however, and it is now kept in the school as a paddle of honour. We hope many more such trophies will be won by our Knights Errant in fair fight for women.

Of all the work in helping women, the hardest is fighting those invisible foes—religious customs. These customs can only change when men learn to respect women, and this respect only comes through knight errantry.

Our staff, of course, have set their faces against early marriage, often having had great trouble in their own families, because they would not marry their own daughters at tender ages. Now, however, we have got a law in Kashmir forbidding early marriage, and our Knights Errant keep their ears and eyes open to hear of any attempted evasions of this law, so as to report them to the police. The law only came into force towards the end of 1928, but within a year our staff were able to prevent one such marriage taking place by informing the police beforehand.

Worse almost than child marriage is enforced widowhood, for no laws can be passed about it, and it depends on public opinion to change this custom.

The lot of Hindu widows is proverbial; one often hears it said that they would be happier if the British had not abolished *suttee*.

Often the widow is without family of her own, and is, therefore, dependent entirely on her late husband's family; her husband being dead, she is at the mercy of the men of the household. She is considered to be the cause of her husband's death, and is, therefore, worthy of any infamy without any rights of redress. Only through the British law has she the right to live. She may never re-marry, though she may be only a child when doomed by widowhood. If, as often happens to one in her helpless plight, she should become a mother, and this fact becomes known to the neighbours, she is considered to have brought disgrace upon the family and is liable to be turned out of the house penniless. However, there are ways of keeping these family secrets hidden, so that a widow may remain on in the house provided nobody ever hears of her lapses.

It was to help these poor unfortunates that our widows' fund was started. A widow, by working hard in her spare time, can spin about seven shillings' worth of wool per month. The staff, therefore, find out any really

THE GUESTS AT THE FIRST RE-MARRIAGE OF HINDU WIDOWS IN SRINAGAR

BOYS GIVING AN AFTERNOON'S OUTING ON THE RIVER TO A PARTY OF CONVALESCENT LADIES

destitute widows, and, on condition that they live moral lives, they offer to pay them the same amount as they earn. This prevents them becoming paupers, and keeps them industrious. This fund is raised by voluntary subscriptions, as far as possible from among the Kashmiris themselves.

For the same reason we founded a masters' benevolent fund, so that our masters' widows should not be left to the tender mercies of the other men in the family. Nobody had ever thought before about making provision for widows.

The following story illustrates what was, and to a large extent still is, the common attitude:

The Principal had to warn one of his staff that the doctor gave him only a few days to live. After breaking the news, he said to the master:

'What provision have you made for your wife and family?'

'I don't know what you mean.'

'What I mean is, what arrangements have you made for your wife and family after you die? Who will take care of them?'

'I don't understand; why should I make arrangements? When I am dead what does it matter who looks after them? I shan't need my wife any more.'

These funds, of course, can only, at best, scratch the surface. The root of the trouble is far deeper down. It lies in the custom of forcing young girls to marry old and diseased men, who are bound to die before many years are over. This leaves countless women in the prime of life without husbands. Since, by Hindu law, no widow may marry again, this means a shortage of women, and that leads to immorality. The shortage of women also means that girls are at once snapped up when they reach marriageable age, and the vicious circle is complete.

The thing is to break the circle by allowing these girl-widows to re-marry. The only difference is, that what is being done now in secret will be done openly and above board. There will be no shame attached to it, and the babies will be allowed to survive.

After many years of trying for this goal, our staff in 1928 managed to bring off the first Hindu widow re-marriage in Srinagar. Fifteen years before this they had tried and very nearly succeeded, but at the last moment the girl had given in, owing to the pressure brought to bear upon her by her religious friends and relations.

On a certain May day in 1928, however, all our staff and about three hundred old boys, who are ex-Knights Errant, were present at a double ceremony, when two widows 'faced the music,' and married two men who had the pluck to marry them. The priests who had promised to perform the ceremony ran away at the last moment, but one of our masters is a priest, and he came forward and did all that had to be done.

Of course, as soon as it had taken place, the orthodox party began to stir up trouble.

A monster meeting was called, to denounce the headmaster and staff and all their wicked ways, in the great Hindu temple near our school. The meeting never came off, however, because one of our old boys, who is in an influential position, warned the governor of the city that there might be somewhat of an uproar. The governor, therefore, ordered the priests of the temple to pay a guarantee of thirty thousand rupees that there would be no unseemly behaviour at the meeting. The priests preferred to keep their cash and have no meeting.

The next year our staff found another destitute girl-widow, who had been turned out of house and home because she was going to have a baby. They took her to hospital, persuaded her to take the step of re-marriage, they found a bridegroom for her, and set her on the road to happiness.

This time the orthodox party confined themselves to a three-day fast, so as to atone for the sins of our staff.

CHAPTER XVII

THE END OF THE CRUISE

HAVING followed the course of the school during its fifty-year voyage against the stream, we have caught up with it and might spend a short time going over it, as it lies at its moorings waiting to launch out again on the next stage of its voyage.

Close to the third bridge of the city stands a tall building on the water's edge, over which flies a flag, on which is worked the device of the crossed paddles and school motto. Here may be seen some six hundred boys, varying in age from five to twenty-five, who form what is called the central school. At various places in the city, smaller buildings, marked by the school crest and motto, accommodate up to a couple of hundred boys in each; these are the branch schools, which draft their boys on to the central school. Another school at Islamabad takes the boys right up to matriculation standard.

A few yards away from the central school is the girls' school. Here the same ideals are set before the future mothers of Kashmir as have been set before the boys. For a long time now, it has been felt that one great block in the way of progress has been the hopeless illiteracy and superstition of the women. Now that this has been tackled, we may hope that our progress up stream will be a far easier job. In years to come we hope that our pupils may be drawn, not only from the children of old boys, but from the children of parents who have *both* come under our influence. These children will start off far ahead of their parents in their outlook and ideals, and we shall hope to forge ahead.

Let us take a look at the central school as it stands to-day. It is an ordinary Kashmiri house, which has been added to from time to time till the buildings have almost encircled a central courtyard. Also the original building has grown considerably in height, till its top classroom, called the pigeon loft, is only outrivalled by the spires of the neighbouring mosques and temples. This room, being high in the air, is devoted to the study of birds, and the master in charge, who is a keen naturalist, is gradually transforming it into a regular aviary of bird pictures.

The buildings are not ideal for a school, as we are very cramped; but, since no European may own any land in Kashmir, we have had to do the best we can in hiring this merchant's house and adapting it to our needs. We are not anxious to add to it more than necessary, for two reasons. Firstly, any additions we make become the property of the landlord; and, secondly, they encroach on the already overcrowded space we have for gymnastics.

So much then for the buildings; now let us take a look at the boys. We will make a start with the kindergarten. In the ordinary course, small boys start their school-life by going to some Hindu or Muhammadan priest, who runs his own private school. We have persuaded some of these schoolmasters to transfer themselves and their scholars into our school, and we give them a salary in proportion to the number of boys they bring. This is the method by which we get most of our boys, for when they get older they are naturally more inclined to stay in the place they know than to go to some strange school.

Here then is the kindergarten, rows of small boys squatting on the ground, with their shoes left outside the door, and with a variety of caps and head coverings on, as is the custom in the East wherever good manners are still observed. These are certainly not a very clean group of little boys, but we cannot be too strict at first, as the parents believe that the devil is especially potent in harming little children who look too attractive and clean. They are mostly wearing that great harbour of disease, the *pheran*, while round their necks hang charms to scare away disease. Even so, there is a limit to the dirt we permit, and if it is overstepped the corrective is to make the little boy become a washerman until such time as he conforms to the necessary standard.

They all sit writing on small blackboards, with reed pens and white paint, or reading in silence; this silence was the cause of a battle in the early days, in which over a hundred boys were removed. The custom of the country in learning is to recite out loud, in a high pitched, monotonous sing-song, while the body is rocked to and fro to the rhythm of this chorus. Imagine the pandemonium when hundreds of boys were indulging in this exercise, and you will see why it had to be abolished at all costs. The parents said that it was impossible to learn in silence; but events have shown that Kashmiri boys can learn, just as well as English boys, even though they learn in silence.

On the walls of this classroom are a number of pictures of animals from different parts of the world. These small boys, of course, cannot understand countries, so we make a start with things they can understand. By grouping the animals geographically, they learn something of how the world varies. A picture of Christ, seated among the children of all nations, introduces them to that about which they will hear more fully later on. Each day they have a practical lesson, in which they draw, prick out and sew with coloured thread on paper, and finally model in clay, various fruits and flowers according to their seasons. This is partly to get them accustomed to using their fingers, and also to try to make them take an interest in everyday things.

Leaving the kindergarten, we go to the next stage, namely, the lower school hall. This hall represents a country, as do all the classrooms from here onwards. The first country of which we wish them to know is, of course, their own country, India. Here, on the walls, are picture post cards from all parts of India, on the north wall is north India, on the south wall south India, and so on. Besides these post cards are glass frames, in which are exhibits which show the preparation or manufacture of common articles of daily use, such as tea, sugar, pens, pencils, or string; all this again is with the object of making them take their minds away from examinations.

Here, as in every classroom, is a picture of some kind action taken from the Gospel story. In this room there are two or three pictures, showing scenes from the childhood of Christ; one of them shows Him as a small boy, carrying a water-pot for His mother, at the well of Nazareth. Mention has already been made in a previous chapter of the women water carriers in Kashmir; this picture is, therefore, especially appropriate, for it gives them straight away an idea of what we mean when we say that Christianity is life and not talk—deeds, not dogma.

Another series of pictures sets forth the life of our King, showing that the head of the Empire gives his life in the service of his subjects; this, we hope, will give them a true outlook in the matter of government service.

Every day, when the lower school boys assemble for roll call and prayers, they face a map of the world showing the British Empire. They see how small a part of that empire Kashmir is, and they learn to be thankful that they are a part of it and enjoy its protection. They know full well the story of the reigns of terror which ravaged their country when it stood weak and friendless. Some day, we hope, Kashmir will not merely be content to take from the empire, but, having become strong, will be able to give of its strength in helping nations less fortunate than itself.

We might pass on through many rooms, having a regular world tour, as the result of seeing the pictures of all nations, which friends in every corner of the world have sent to us. The beautiful posters of the British Empire Marketing Board, and those issued by railway and travel agencies, almost give one the impression of being in an underground railway station in London. In this account, however, we must take all that for granted, and only pause to look at one or two things of special interest.

From the lower school hall we pass into the upper school hall. Here we have on the walls large boards, on which are the names of those whom we wish to honour. On one board are the names of those who have shown special grit—for example, those who have swum across the Wular or jumped into the river from the school roof, fifty feet. On another board are the names of those who won the medal which Lord Lansdowne presented to the school on the occasion of his visit. This medal is awarded to the boy who is voted by his fellows to have best upheld the traditions of his school in body, mind, and soul. We never find that the voting goes on communal lines, for Christians, Hindus and Muhammadans have all received this honour.

The boy who does the bravest deed of the year in saving life has his name painted in letters of gold on another board; while the boy who does the kindest deed of the year to animals has his name remembered as an example to his fellows.

Lastly, we come to the board of greatest honour, placed at the end of the hall, so that all the boys may see it when they assemble in the morning. There are the names of those who have given their lives for others; over the board is a crown and under it a picture of Christ. Without talk, that is a daily object lesson. There is the Inspiration, there is the Example, there is the essence of the teaching which Christ gave His life to hand on to them. Round this board we hang pictures of noble men and women who have given their lives in the service of others. There is Captain Oates, of the Antarctic; Edith Cavell; Dr. Arthur Neve, who lived and died in Kashmir, so that its people might have healthy bodies and healthy souls; there also is Dr. Pennel, of the Afghan frontier; and also that valiant man of

Kashmir, Samuel Bakkal. This last was one of themselves, a Kashmiri who, while a boy in this school, confessed his faith in Christ; he was starved, beaten and even tied to a cross, but he won through and lived to be a veritable Joseph to his people during the years which followed the famine mentioned in a previous chapter.[1] There before them on that wall is the ideal; and more than that, there are those who have followed that ideal to the end, proving that it is not an impossible ideal with such a Leader.

From this hall we go out into the playground to see the daily gymnastic period. A bugle blows, and out of windows, down shutes and poles, a cascade of three hundred boys pours out in twenty-five seconds. They are soon lined up, the band strikes up, and for ten minutes they go through mass drill in time to the strains of the band. They then break up into squads and double off to their various special turns for the day—it may be boxing, fencing, jumping, bars or ropes, etc. Each day the squads move on, so that every boy has a try at everything; after ten minutes of this, they again form up, and stand still, while a short prayer is offered for the King, the Viceroy and the Maharajah, and the government of their empire and country. The band then plays the National Anthem, followed by the Kashmir anthem, while the whole school salutes the flags which are simultaneously hoisted. After this everyone stands still for one minute in silence, while they remember boys in all parts of the Empire growing up to become useful citizens. Again the band strikes up, and they all double off for a ten minutes' recess before returning to their classrooms.

Scattered all over the school, in conspicuous places, are mottos of various kinds; for example, over the door leading to the masters' common room, there is this most necessary hint for avoiding petty jealousies: 'Do thy best, but rejoice with him that doeth better.' Over another door the words, 'Be Prepared,' indicate the Scout room. During recent years a small troop of Scouts has been formed in the school, affiliated to the world-wide movement started by Lord Baden Powell. Care is taken in selecting from those boys who ask to be enrolled only those who are considered to have an idea of the meaning of the word *honour*. We wish to preserve this splendid brotherhood from any taint or stigma, as far as it lies within our power. Our Scout troop differs slightly from the usual, in that it has

[1] A fuller account of the life of Samuel Bakkal may be found in *A Valiant Man of Kashmir*, by Rev. C. E. Tyndale-Biscoe, published by C.M.S. Salisbury Square, London, E.C. 4. Price, one penny.

a green uniform instead of khaki; this is because they are the Kashmir counterpart of Sea Scouts. They are Lake and River Scouts, and, therefore, have a uniform which blends with the reeds of the lakes.

Nearly all Kashmiri houses have very low doors. The reason for this is not that the Kashmiris are small of stature, but it dates from the days of the Afghan rule. The haughty Afghan conquerors were in the habit of riding into Kashmiri homes on horseback, stabling their horses in the lower rooms and occupying the rest for themselves. Being unable to prevent these outrages by force, the Kashmiris devised the cunning plan of having such low doors that, not only must the intruder dismount, but he must also bow the head on entry. No Afghan would willingly make obeisance to a Kashmiri, so he must perforce remain outside; that, at any rate, is the legend.

In the old original parts of the school are these same low doorways. Over the lowest of these doors, which leads to the Principal's small office, is the legend, 'Humility.' Everyone going through that door, except a small boy, must be very humble, or receive a sharp rap across the forehead.

In this same small study hang two other mottos. When a boy stands before the Principal for the last time, before leaving the school, the first of these two mottos is pointed to him, and he reads 'Honesty is the best policy, but not yet in Kashmir.' During his time in the school, he has perhaps learnt something of honour and honesty. He now has to go into a different world with different standards, and that motto is to warn him of what he may expect to find. Perhaps he protests that he will run straight, or perhaps he says that he will try to run straight; then the Principal points out to him the second motto, 'Trust in God.' That alone can keep him straight, or help to keep him straight, for there is no one else who will help him once he leaves the protecting influence of his school for the troubled waters of life, where from henceforth he must paddle his own canoe upstream.

Thus we leave the school to push on its way once more. As each year goes by, more and more solitary canoes, whose occupants first learnt how to fight against the stream while in this boat whose course we have followed, are manfully fighting upwards; while others, finding the pace too hard, drop back and drift, as their fathers drifted before them.

Let us hope that, when the time comes for telling the story of the

THE C.M.S. HIGH SCHOOL TROOP OF LAKE AND RIVER SCOUTS

MEN IN THE MAKING

THE GIANTS' STRIDE, WHERE SMALL BOYS MAKE A START IN ACQUIRING MUSCLE

POLE JUMPING OVER A LIVING HURDLE

PHYSICAL JERKS ON THE HEAD

next fifty years against the stream, it will be possible to say that, owing to the efforts of the solitary canoes, the first motto in the Principal's study will have ceased to be true; while perhaps, who knows, but that the second may have become true through the greater part of Kashmir.

A Typical Page from the Citizenship Book, Showing One Day's Activity in the Social Service Line

JUNE 17, 1929

Upper School

D Company (IV H, III M, II M, I M) under Munshi Neranjan Nath	Took out eleven patients from the hospital.
Janki Nath Mattu (I MB) ..	Put a young crow back into its nest.
Prithvi Nath (I MB)	Carries water for his mother.
Rahman Sheikh (III MA) ..	Helped an old woman in carrying a bag of shali from Habba Kadal Ghat to Kania Kadal.

Rainawari School

Master Shanker Pandith and a party of boys	Took eight patients from Mission Hospital to Dal Lake.

Amira Kadal School

Abdul Aziz (V P) .. Mohamed Shah (V P) ..	Helped a small boy by carrying his rice, about 30 seers, from Drugjan Bridge to Buchwara.

Nawa Kadal School

Mohamed Dar (V P)	Helped a woman by carrying a water-pot from the tap to her house.
Masters Nila Kanth and Dina Nath and a party of boys ..	Took out forty-three patients from the Diamond Jubilee Zenana Hospital for an airing in four *shikaras*.

Haba Kadal School

A party of twelve boys ..	Pushed a failed motor car from Chandmari to Amira Kadal.
Jagar Nath (V P)	Helped an old woman by carrying a bag of shali from Habba Kadal to Shahli Teng.

Red School

Mahinder Nath (IV P).. ..	Finding a log floating down the Kuta Kul, near Mr. Avery's sawing machine, took off his clothes, swam, and, with the help of another boy of upper school, brought it back to the bank and tied it there.
Balabader (IV P)	Led a little boy, who had lost his way, from Kani Kadal to Zaindar Mohalla to his house.

Note.—The symbols in brackets merely indicate the boys' forms.

THE SCHOOL HONOUR BOARDS

1. To Those Who Have Risked Their Lives for Others

1899.	Bagwan Das Bala Koul Suraj Raina Shankar Pandith Vishna Koul	Ran great risk in cholera epidemic.
1900.	Shanker Koul	A very weak swimmer, saved a school-fellow.
1903.	Mahdu Bat	Saved two boys at the same time.
1904.	Tarak Bat	Saved an old woman, nearly dead from heat and smoke, in the big fire at Amira Kadal.
1906.	Wasa Dive	Aged 15, saved a school-fellow, aged 13, from drowning in the Jhelum.
1907.	Hasan Sheik Noor Nakash	Aged 11 and 12, saved a boy, aged 17, from drowning in the Jhelum.
1908.	Mahamud Zerger	Saved two children from a burning house.
1909.	Noor Din	Saved a child from drowning.
1910.	Dina Nath	Saved a girl from drowning.
1911.	Aftab Pandith	Saved a Hindu school-boy from the whirlpool at the Dal Gate.
1913.	Salam Khan	Saved an American lady from drowning in the river at night.
1914.	Shambu Nath	Saved a boy from drowning in the river.
1915.	Nand Lal	Saved a boy, aged 12, from drowning in the swirl at Haba Kadal Bridge.
1916.	Rada Krishen Koul	Saved three lives from drowning.
	Jis Lal Kak	Saved a boy from drowning.
1917.	Rada Krishen Pir	Saved a boy, almost his own age, from drowning.
	Amir Wani	Saved a man's life from a powerful electric shock.
1918.	Kant Pandith	Saved a mad man and a blind man at the same time from drowning in the Rainawari Canal.
1919.	Gopi Nath Saraf	Saved two women from drowning in the Dal Lake.
1920.	Shaban Bat	Leapt from the school roof and saved a boy who had sunk in the river.
1921.	Rhago Dhar	Saved a girl from drowning in the Jhelum.
1922.	Sirwanand Bhan	Twice saved lives from drowning.
1923.	Shaban Bat	Saved three lives from drowning during the year.
1924.	Ghulam Mohamed	Saved two boys from drowning in the river.
1925.	Abdul Malik	Saved a girl, aged 5, from drowning in the Tsunti Kul Canal.

Year	Name	Deed
1926.	Rishi Loan	Saved a boy from drowning in the lake when men feared to go to the rescue.
	Subhan Ganai	
	Nand Lal Bakaya	Saved the lives of two ladies and a gentleman, at Kana Kadal.
	Gulam Mahomed	
1927.	Lasa Khan	Saved three women and a child from a capsized boat, near Ali Kadal Bridge.
	Sona Sheik	
1928.	Amar Khan	Dived twice under a houseboat to save a drowning boy.
1929.	Rajab Bat	Killed single-handed a mad dog, which had bitten six people.

2. The Kindest Deed of the Year to Animals

Year	Name	Deed
1906.	Bagwan Dass	Saved a dying donkey from birds of prey.
1907.	Sirwanand	Saved a dog from drowning in a well.
1908.	Eight boys	Saved five cows from a burning house.
1909.		One hundred donkeys saved from starvation by the boys during the year.
1911.	Govind Bhan	Saved a drowning dog.
1912.	Radha Krishen	Took a dog out of a well.
	Tara Chand	Saved a dying pony from birds of prey.
1913.	Mahadive Pandith	Took a dog from a well.
	Vishna Hakim	Saved a pony with a broken leg from a cruel death.
	Bagwan Dass	
1915.	Suraj Raina	Removed the load from a lame pony and made the driver carry the load.
1916.	Bagwan Dass	Saved a dying pony from birds of prey.
1917.	Rugh Nath	Saved a pony from a well.
1918.	Bagwan Dass	Delivered a lame pony with sore back from its load.
1919.	Mahisha Koul	Saved a donkey in the snow from starvation.
	Tota Koul	Gave food and lodging to a starving cow for three days.
1920.	Priam Nath	Took a bone out of a dog's throat.
1921.	Vishna Hakim	Saved several tonga ponies from cruel treatment.
1923.	Janki Nath Koul	Saved a puppy from drowning in blood.
1924.	Ahad Dar	Extracted a bone from a dog's throat.
1925.	Tara Chand Gunju	Went down a deep well at night and pulled out a dog.
1926.	Jagar Nath Nagri	Extracted bones out of two pariah dogs' throats.
	Gulam Mohamed	
1927.	Jaffer Meer	Saved a dog from drowning in a deep well.
1928.	Ahad Dar	Rescued two ponies from a flooded stable.
1929.	Jagar Nath	Brought coals and freed a mina, which had become frozen to a tap on which it had perched.

FUTURE LIFE SAVERS

THE DAILY SWIMMING LESSON

400 BOYS TAUGHT TO SWIM IN ONE YEAR, WITH THEIR TEACHERS

SMALL BOYS LEARNING TO SWIM

THOSE WHO RISKED THEIR LIVES FOR OTHERS IN 1929

3. To Those Who Have Given Their Lives for Others

1898.	Mahishur Koul ..	Lost his life in saving his brother from drowning.
1917.	Rev. H. O. Robertson	Killed in France.
	Mohamed Din ..	2nd Kashmir Infantry. Killed in East Africa.
	Bhag Ali	3rd Kashmir Rifles. Killed in East Africa.
	Perth Singh ..	Lance Naik. Killed in East Africa.
1922.	Mahanand Razdan ..	Gave his life, after nursing seven of his household during typhus.
1929.	S. Chimed Gergen ..	Murdered by kuth smugglers at Zanskar, and gave his life for the purity of public service.

MAP OF KASHMIR VALLEY AND JHELUM VALLEY ROAD

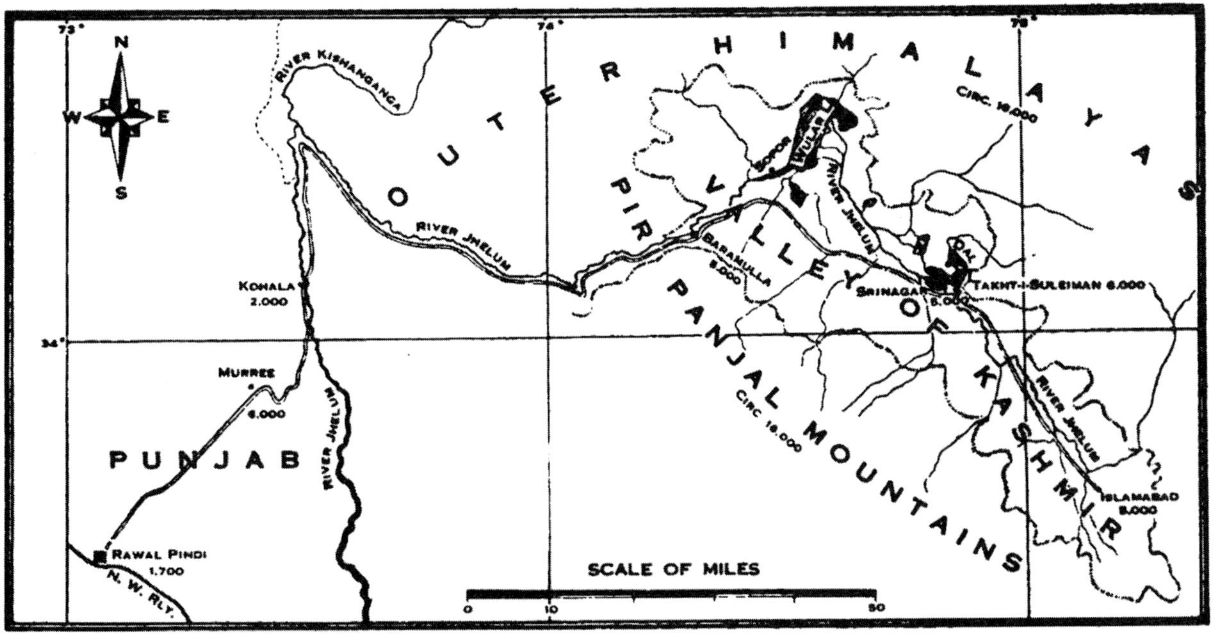

APPENDIX

List of Those Connected with the School

	Rev. J. S. Doxey	1878–1880
Founder and Principal	Rev. J. H. Knowles	1880–1901
Principal	Rev. C. E. Tyndale-Biscoe	1890–
Headmaster	K. P. Sircar	1891–1895
Vice-Principal	G. W. Tyndale-Biscoe	1896–1902
Technical Instructor	A. B. Tyndale	1899–1901
	Rev. C. L'E. Burges	1899–1901
	Rev. C. E. Barton	1900–1902
Acting-Principal	Rev. Marcus Wigram	1903–1904
Vice-Principal	Rev. F. E. Lucey	1904–1921
Headmaster	Shenker Koul, Master and Boy	from 1892–
Short Service	C. F. Hall	1904–1905
Vice-Principal, Islamabad	Miss Coverdale	1907–1927
Short Service	C. Musgrave	1911–1912
Short Service	O. H. Robertson	1911–1913
Short Service	S. T. Gray	1913–1914
	Samuel Bakkal	1913–1914
Vice-Principal	Rev. J. S. Dugdale	1920–1927
Short Service	R. Denton Thompson	1925–1927
Vice-Principal, Islamabad	H. C. Guyer, O.B.E.	1927–1928
Vice-Principal	E. D. Tyndale-Biscoe	1927–

Medical Advisers

Dr. Kate Knowles	1907–1915
Dr. S. Wilson	1916–1924
Dr. Mathewson	1925–1926
Dr. Dina Nath	1926–

Girls' School

Miss Violet Fitze	1910–1920
Miss F. A. Mackay	1910–1911
Mrs. J. S. Dugdale	1920–1927
Miss M. Mallinson	1922–
Miss Ahmad Shah	1924–
Miss Mosse	1925–1926
Miss Price	1928–1929
Miss B. James	1929–

Voluntary and Part-time Helpers

Bomford, Rev. T.
Burges, Miss H. L'E.
Churchill Taylor, Miss
Fellowes, Mrs. J. R.
Greville Stuart, Mrs.
Joyce, H. C.
Kay, Rev. A. I.
Lamb, Rev. G. H.
Langdale-Smith, Miss D.
McCormick, Miss L.
Neve, Mrs. Arthur
Osmaston, Miss
Paterson, Rev. J. M.
Petrie, Miss Irene
Russell, Miss Evelyn
Stanton, Rev. H. U. W.
Stubbs, Miss
Tyndale-Biscoe, Mrs. C. E.
Tyndale-Biscoe, Mrs. E. D.
Webb, Miss K.

Gymnastic Instructors

Colonel Dempster
S. W. Steane
Major K. C. Hadow

Honorary Treasurer

C. M. Hadow

INDEX